Contents

Editorial

Click here for the truth about *Gutter*. The so-called Magazine of New Scottish Writing is in fact a secret project of the global metropolitan elite to distract the vulnerable hardworking people of Scotland and elsewhere from the real job of paying taxes to their country. Instead, the evil editors at *Gutter* tempt wannabes with empty promises of publication and a free two-year subscription. They can't even pay a proper fee because they keep all that massive, taxpayer-funded profit for THEMSELVES!

Once hooked, these manipulators simply steal other people's writing and distribute it in their so-called magazine, which in fact nobody reads. Their distraction complete, these one-time reliable workers forget about their duty to this great democracy of ours and indulge themselves in gross fantasies of success and fame.

So in love with themselves are these *Gutter* people that they try to create a "safe space" for new writing and use fancy foreign words like *milieu* and *zeitgeist* without a hint of irony. We think there should be no safe space for these fakers, they need to get back to making real entertainment for the people, people like you and me. Alternatively they should find themselves a real job. Let's see how these fat cat editors and authors fare on the minimum wage.

If you want proof, just look at this current issue where they publish writing from a bunch of folks from France. France! What has France ever done for our great culture here? The land of croissants, wine and socialism has also produced some of the worst books ever seen on this planet, written by a bunch of self-loathing idiots like Marcel Proust, Emile Zola, Jean-Paul Sartre, Albert Camus, Charles Baudelaire, Paul Verlaine, to name a few. It is proof, if proof were needed that they too are part of a secret conspiracy to ignore the clear will of the people at last year's referendum and keep this country in the clutches of the European Union. By showing you this mistranslated "writing" from a foreign culture, what they want is for you to think, "oh, maybe those poor French are just like us", we'd be better off staying with them. But they aren't like us, don't fall for it! Their EU actually wants to take more and more of our writing and this magazine is part of a devilish plan to help them get it. We won't get anything in return except red tape around our books. In fact, by NOT reading this issue of *Gutter* you will ensure an extra 350 million words a week stay in the UK to help our National Health Service.

Enough! It's exhausting. We can't sustain the vitriol for more than five hundred words. Our point is hopefully made though: if you find yourself asking what now for fiction and poetry in a post-truth age where news is fiction, then one answer is to make fiction and poetry the news! Sharpen those satirical pencils friends, and poke them at the numpties who are leading the US and Europe into the abyss of insularity, protectionism, reaction and intolerance. Engage with people who vehemently disagree. Most importantly, do your research, check your facts, highlight the ridiculous. Your voice has never been more necessary.

There are dangers here, however: if you make your satire too perfectly Swiftian, then it may not be read as such by people who are somewhat hard-of-thinking. While the first section of this Editorial is far from *A Modest Proposal...*, we imagine it's only a matter of time before some libertarian idiot references it on Breitbart as "evidence" against public funding of literary magazines.

But we are only fictioneers and poets, our best hope is that we can reflect society and perhaps change it one mind at a time. Maybe a better chance rests with journalists themselves, they once had an audience reach that we writers could only dream of, and perhaps their time has come again? Over Christmas, *Gutter* found itself having lunch with childhood friends, both of whom are journalists and reviewers of some years' experience and repute. We put it to them that proper journalism now has a call to arms: against the fake news stories overrunning the Internet and social media. An honourable idea, they felt, but with the newspaper sector so decimated by free news sites, resources so stretched, the battle may already be lost. So, our other request to you is to subscribe to and support your journalism of choice, comment on comments pages, check facts, engage differing views.

From the real world back to life imagined: with this issue, we are delighted to continue the international flavour of Issue 15 with fiction and poetry from and about France. Our decision to do so predates last June's events, and was intended as a celebration of European writing and the Auld Alliance. Along with other polemic poetry found between pages 109-128, it now forms our collective two fingers at the Brexiting establishment. Shamefully little writing is translated into our languages from the continent, and it has always been our mission at *Gutter* (and Freight Books) to do our small part to rectify that situation.

On p. 165 is a new Scots version, 'Unsicht', of Guy de Maupassant's 'l'Aveugle'. Written by James Robertson – who is making a welcome, and long-overdue, début in *Gutter* – its bleak and emotive tale is told in an accessible free translation.

Continuing with minority languages, we have a fascinating five-way translation of five poems by Aurelia Lassaque from her native French and Occitan via the English of James Thomas, into the Shetlandic and Orcadian Scots of Christie Williamson & Harry Giles respectively. Watch how the languages mutate, and if you are a cognate-geek you will be enthralled for hours. The 'full set' can be found on our website.

Other pieces of French writing that we are proud to present include 'The Lady of Cyrus' by the esteemed French-Lebanese writer Vénus Khoury-Ghata, and the long poem 'Metropole Oubliée' by Benjamin Guérin – the French original of which is on our website. Elsewhere, on page 121 you can see Lou Sarabadzic's delightful explorations of French in English and English in French, and on page 005 AC Clarke's translation of Paul Edwards 'Pour Vivre Ici'.

Bridging the Atlantic theme of the last issue with the Francophone theme of this one, we have a two way translation between Edinburgh-based Northern Irish poet Rachel McCrum and her Québécois partner Jonatham Lamy. Rachel is also the subject of the Gutter Interview on page 067.

As well as the much reported death of truth in 2016, the past year also saw a lot of deaths of beloved public figures in the arts and entertainment. Following the massive growth of popular culture from the mid 20th century onwards, we are now entering an era when those icons and pioneers are entering old age and dying. This scent of death and ageing seemed to permeate the submissions pile for Issue 16. But getting old doesn't mean you can't have a good-looking, sexually-active Late Middle Age, as Liz Lochhead's charming exhortation to do the 'Salsa Geriatrica' (p.007) shows us. We also have two beautiful epithalamions from the old romantic on p. 061 later, on pg. 064, Tom Pow reflects on childhood, past love and existence with 'The Champion' and 'Clear Out'.

We were honoured to receive three poems by the wonderful DM Black. We are very glad that he has chosen *Gutter* to air his new pieces.

We also welcome an array of lesser-known poetic talents to this issue, including Nuala Watt, Stuart A Paterson, Diana Hendry, Gillian Mellor and Rachel Plummer. Thank you to all the other poets for a great set of submissions for us to choose from.

Prose highlights include the gruesome 'Bernice' by Andrew Murray Scott, followed by the equally murderous stories 'Hobbies in Retirement' by Elissa Soave and 'Baron's Basement' by the acclaimed historical crime writer Shona Maclean. We are also grateful to Doug Johnston for the curiously titled 'Moby Dickheads', while the maritime flavour is given a twist by Shane Strachan's 'Quines at Sea'.

If you enjoyed this issue, please consider taking out a subscription to support new writing. Think of it as karma. A subscription also makes a perfect gift for a friend or lover. See www.guttermag.co.uk for details.

The Drummer

DM Black

The man with the bass guitar is wearing a dark purple hat,
and the saxophonist is wearing a dress
that might have intrigued Mondrian,
but the drummer, who is mixed-race
or perhaps of some unexpected ethnicity like, shall we say, Javan,
wears the face of an angel. He gazes rapt at the guitarist,
clearly in love, and he seems to have quite forgotten
that he is supposed to be part of this band, if he is, and perhaps he isn't,
perhaps I'm mistaken, and he smiles
dreamily, seraphically, as his hands wander among the cymbals
or smash his sticks on the drums and his feet pedal ceaselessly –
but his life is all in his face, his loving lazy
beautiful face that he turns towards the guitarist, ignoring
his unerring members as they
caress and thrash among the drum-kit, turning its order
into a forest of din tormented by lightning-flashes and thunder-claps
– near him, it must be admitted, but clearly in no way his responsibility.

The White Car

DM Black

I had allowed myself to believe
that it was a special grade of white
('pearlescent orchid' the manufacturer called it)

that would not show the dirt;
and in this pleasant state of illusion
continued for several months

to see no dirt
(though 'isn't it time you washed the car?' my wife said to me)
– seeing only

pearlescent orchid. Today, emptying
bucket after bucket
of grimy soap-foam

into the gridded drain and squeezing out abundant
cloths and sponges,
I was reminded

of an early experience
of psychotherapy
with a smiling, pearlescent

once-beautiful woman on whom
nothing appeared to stick.
Fortunately the resemblance

ended before the outcome,
which in the case of the car
was perfectly satisfactory –

for the car was merely white
and it was only I who had thought it
'pearlescent orchid'.

A Voice over the Tannoy

DM Black

'You will remember on leaving the submarine
that your eyes have become accustomed
to extremely near horizons,
and that though you have remained acquainted
with the wider world, the periscope
gave only a restricted perspective
on a scene lacking several of the dimensions
that now confront you.
These are just facts.
You should not hold yourself responsible for them.

'You have been hyper-alert
to a very small array of signals,
not one of which will now flash, bleep, or unfold itself
in the huge daylight surrounding you.
You remember daylight, of course,
with its peculiar absence of boundaries:
it now shows you the disordered rocks,
the lip of foam, and the hills,
and the slipway running down into the black seaweed.
You will feel an emotion like fear
at your lack of confinement.
That is entirely understandable.

'It is also understandable
that you will feel critical
of the civilians you will encounter – in the harbour first, then in the de-briefing sheds,
later, still more, in the village –
you will be struck by their languor and lack of briskness.
They will seem to you half-asleep
and not agents in their own right but appendages of indeterminate groupings,
distracted by matters not worth attending to.
This is because they are civilians.
All your reactions are normal.

'Another thing: where you have come from
you have been important:
though of low rank
your work was essential,
for a crew is an engine,
no part of it is redundant.
No officer succeeds
if he fails to care for each man,
and to have each man care for each other.
I use the word "care"
in the strongest possible sense:
this is not a matter of mere surface appearances.
Where you are going, whim prevails;
whim, inclination, fantasy:
they should not be despised;
they have built civilisations,
but it is hard to know what weight you can put on them,
hard, too, to know them for what they are.
There are women too, who are often attractive –
but that's a big subject;
if you take my advice you will keep yourself to yourself,
at least for the time being.

'You should reckon it will take nine months at a minimum
to adapt yourself to civilian life,
and you should not expect to do so entirely:
strangeness will always remain part of the package.

'So, good luck, Jimmy!
You step alone through the hatch

'but those who watch are all rooting for you:
every man jack of us in the fullness of time
will take the same exit'

To live here (Pour Vivre Ici)

Paul Éluard
(translated from the French by *AC Clarke*)

The sky having deserted me, I made a fire
a fire to be a friend
a fire to enter into the night of winter
a fire to live better.

I gave it what day had given me
forests, bushes, cornfields, vines
nests and their birds, houses and their keys
insects, flowers, furs, celebrations.

I lived with only the noise of crackling flames
with only the smell of their heat;
I was like a boat sinking in an inland sea
like a dead man I had only one element.

The Department of Work and Pensions Assesses a Jade Fish.

Nuala Watt

Once, I held three thousand pale green years.

Should I compare myself to the jade fish?

I am in a museum of difficulties.
I feature in a national catalogue.
Handled, but not with care.

Juliet. Echo.
One. Five. Zero.
Treble Two.
C. That's me.

I'm a fraudster who walks.

Tick this box. Tick this box. Tick this box. Now.

How often do you lose consciousness?
Exactly how much of your life is a mess?

Can you make a cup of tea?

We cannot pay you.

The law says. The law says. The law says.
The phone squanders an hour.
This is because you have as much or more...

By the power of brown envelopes
I miss my class on poetics:
'Imagine The Voices of Things'.

The Dirty Diva Attempts to Invent a New Dance Craze

Liz Lochhead

Can't get my socks on
Can't get my rocks off
But that loss of libido
That everybody talks of
Is yet to kick in

Let's do the Salsa Geriatrica
It's
No sin

There are those
God knows
Think at Our Age it's
Not Right
Never ever play
Their Marvin Gaye
Their Lay, Lady Lay,
Nor their
Barry White...
I'm like Oh give it a spin
Let's *try* the Salsa Geriatrica
It's
No sin

Jeepers creepers
The Grim Reaper
For crying out loud
He's cutting a cruel swathe
Through the Old Crowd.
He's on the rampage!
So what we gonna do
With our Late Middle Age?

Try it on with
Some septuagenarians
And they go: Gie's peace!
They're like: I'm glad I'm past it, it's
A Merciful Release.
Me? I'm like
Get Ready, Get set, Begin
The Salsa Geriatrica!
It's
No Sin.

Had we but world enough
And time
Pro-crastination
Were no crime...
But
Unless the whole idea's
Totally horrendous – or (worse!) *risible* --
Delay is inadvisable
At our age.
Are we on the same page?
What *else* we gonna do with our
Late Middle Age.

The Roe Deer

Gordon Meade

Today, we saw, not a rabbit
in the headlights, but a roe deer
leaping from one side of the road
to another in front of our car.

By the time we had talked
about how wonderful it had been
to have seen it, it was already halfway across the adjacent field.

That is the sort of getaway
I am after; speed, grace and power.
When the time comes, I want to
be able to cross over with

the same ease as that deer.
Even before I have been missed,
it is my intention to be already halfway across the adjacent field.

Ending

William Bonar

I

Properties to let in dingy streets,
up closes of cat pee,
chip fat, cabbage stench;

flats, smelling of dust,
smoke, old sweat; rooms
full of wasted time, loss.

This is the wrong part
of town to make a break,
to take a chance.

The breeze is cooling,
a hint of rain.
Some wounds are too deep.

She makes light, mocking,
as if cajoling a child
who'd run away;

as if there'd been no shouting;
as if the sick, pale thing
needed only a bandage, aspirin.

Some wounds are too deep.

II

Thirty years. Next year, it's thirty.
It cannot be countenanced.
It cannot be celebrated with
an obscenely expensive meal in
an award-winning restaurant.

Thread-bare conversation
across immaculate napery.

Silent flunkies on hand assessing
every desperate gesture,
every unguarded flicker of boredom,
contempt. Each specimen
of the poor pale thing,
squirming in stainless steel,
taken for vivisection.

III
There was time, of course,
when it thrived, it grew.
Time when it might bear.

Lost now. Was there
always a flaw — the wrong
genes — a wrong match —

ovum and sperm
misconceived — a bloody
mess in a toilet pan?

No, there was time.
There was. There was
time to grow. Time

to slide, to stale,
to remember slights.
Time
                to forget
                        kindness.

IV

It could be a narrow street
dark tenements on either side
no lights   none in the windows
closes black as the mouths of hell

Then a flat   familiar but the lights
don't work   no one is there   the rooms
multiply   each beyond the last

Something is there   in pursuit
closing in   you're running
winding stairs   more rooms
empty rooms   dark   empty rooms
you sense its cold breath   try to call out but
no sound comes   no sound comes
you're running on sand
it's closing   closing   no sound
frantic   forced air makes moan
forced limbs   forced air makes shout

You lie in sweat   terror slinks away
like a kicked dog   casting
sleekit backward looks   *Catch you*
next time   I'll catch you next time

V

Did we think, if the poor
pale thing left that big house
filled with stuff, it might thrive again?

In leaving we paused, shared
our shame. Then turned
the key, expelled ourselves.

And the sickness went with us.
No fruit not bitter.
No knowledge a cure.

VI

Now is the killing time.
Over tea
at a blue table.

Now as the sun
begins its slow
decline   sacrifice.

A handful of words
and the poor, pale
thing is dead.

Like actors improvising
while the prompt
finds his place,

we know what
to do when
the line is delivered.

We know the rites.

I take a peek at him behind my shades and say thank you nicely, another middle-aged, unshaved, unlovely old buzzard, red wrinkled neck, jug-ears sticking out under a blue baseball cap. Yep, just like my daddy. They could be fucken twins.

Bernice

Andrew Murray Scott

Bernice

Andrew Murray Scott

Fifty yards out they see me standing just out of town. They drop gears, air hisses out of cylinder brakes and I see them high up, craning ahead like tortoises, through the polarised glass, eyes out on stalks. Is the dame alone? Is there a boyfriend hiding behind her? But the rigs scrape to a halt fifty yards on – *chance too good to miss anyhow* – and I see them check me in the high side mirrors as I scamper legs akimbo, hauling that awkward holdall towards the snorting leviathan that trembles under their dirt-stained hands. They always lean over to help me in with a hairy paw and have a good leer at my legs, the black pvc miniskirt, loose teeshirt, maybe no bra underneath... They're hopin.

Yeah, even fifty yards out, their reptile brains is squirming wondering if I'm real – or a fantasy. The kind of lies they get from the greasy skin mags piled up under the aluminium bucket seats. It's like – I've gotta be there for them – they can't conceive it to be otherwise. Too much a coincidence for it to be anything else. Like somebody waved a fucken wand or something. I'm a princess in two dimensions. On one side, I'm beautiful (they guess), on the flip side I must be available. Because I look sexy, it's gotta happen. They expect.

So this guy, this latest in a long line, fetches over and hands me a beer from a cooler in back. I take a peek at him behind my shades and say thank you nicely, another middle-aged, unshaved, unlovely old buzzard, red wrinkled neck, jug-ears sticking out under a blue baseball cap. Yep, just like my daddy. They could be fucken twins. Fifty, maybe older, baggy J-Mart jeans, stinks of sweat and engine oil. Black grit under the mashed fingernails as he handed me the beer and nervously I guess wiped his lips with the back of that meaty paw. I can see everything, a delapidated trailer-home in some nowhere suburb of San Antonio, a curdled wife ballooning out her velour track-pants. All day long sittin on her fanny eating chips and watching the networked soaps, one kid in the army, the other gone wrong, pointless, wasted life. Human vegetables, like stinking mushrooms, this guy's going nowhere except the next delivery depot.

'Wanna smoke, babe?' he mumbles through gritted teeth. It's like he don't wanna lose no precious air by opening his mouth, which is like a lizard's, tight and slitty. His eyes is doing all the work, darting over my face, at my front and down at my legs, making no secret what he's thinking.

'Hell, sure is hot!' I see the sweat starting on his flabby face. I'm exciting him just by being here. He licks his thin dry lips and exhales blue smoke from his nostrils. Hairy nostrils, just like my pa's. Just like I used to see every night, close up. From underneath. Every night ma was out. Ya alright honey, Ya not hurtin? Wouldn't wanna hurt daddy's li'l girl... and the same smell of dust and oil and sweat.

Highway 70 now, she cuts diagonally down across Arizona, and there sure ain't nothing to see, empty desert, dry clay, white sand and muffled blurred shapes that gotta be scrub bushes or cactus shadows. You don't make no shadows here an anythin that moves is just a blur at the corner of your eye. This is as far as I could get. I'll get gone further just give me time. I wanna be so far nobody can see me or get me back.

His mouth's moving. I hear: 'What's your name, honey?'

I still don't expect to hear words, not real voices that're not inside my head. Seem too loud somehow to be real, like I'm imagining it. It's been four weeks now. My ears still ain't adjusted to, like, talking and such.

'Uh?' He's lookin at me so I slup some beer, wipe my lips, take my time. 'I'm Bernice,' I tell him. *My sister. She got out early. She knew the bastard he was. All men.*

'Sweet name', he says without expression. 'You're real lucky ah stopped,' he turns and opens his mouth at me, a sort-of lopsided grin. His teeth are brown at the roots. 'Company don't allow no riders,' he says. He stabs the front of his check-shirt with the ball of his thumb. 'Out here I'm ma own boss.' He looks over, eyes narrowed, hesitating. He's chewed it over an decided I gotta be a hooker. 'Y'don't look like no ordinary rider. Hell, you don't,' he quavers kind of nervous and the back of his hairy hand comes up to wipe the blue line of his lips. 'We don't get many of your type down here. Why... ah guess you rides just about anything down the road? Hot damn! Any old dawg that just comes along?' He tries a laugh – he ain't got the breath - and that makes it even more embarrassing. He leers at my legs and starts fidgetting at his crotch. 'Guess ah ain't wrong honey? Sweet jaybirds – ma ass – you'd be a workin girl, I reckon, huh?'

'Maybe, but you can't afford me.' I let the tin go out the window. Then I wind her back up again. Good reason not to look at him. I know what's coming.

'Huh? Huh? Guess ah kin cover any price ya name. You call it. Darlin, you look good enough to eat up. We can go right here, in back.' He slaps the bunk behind us. 'Ain't no-one gonna know. Why, hell,' he finishes tamely, 'I hate the company tellin' me what ah can and caint do.'

I say nothing. There's silence for a minute or two. I see that's he's already unzipped his jeans. 'What you saying, honey?' he asks after another moment or two.

'Nothin' personal,' I say. 'I been travelling awhile, mister. I ain't about to get kicked out in the middle o' nowhere soon as you had your kicks.'

'Aw, cutie, you got the wrong guy. I ain't gonna give you no bad time. Why, I'd take mighty good care a you'.

'You say.' I make the mistake of looking down, which is what he wanted, I guess.

'There's a lot a rough guys out here, hon. Copper-mining country. Why – it's apache land, hell, them injuns over the San Carlos Reservation would have them your skimpy white pantees off soon's look at ya. Ya wouldn't never see no money neither. You sure lucky ah stopped, babe. Anyhow, what can I do that aint already bin done to you? I'm just lookin for a bit of fun, hon.'

'I gotta get to Safford, that's all I know. You going to get me there?'

'Why sure honey, of course I can get ya there. Ah can drop ya anywheres you say.' He grins, relieved. 'Safford, huh? Then you'll go in back with me?'

'Maybe.'

'Aw, honey...' I feel his rough fingers slide over my thigh and slip up under the skirt. I push them away. 'We ain't at Safford, mister.'

The road rolls on, climbing to Gonzalez Pass, 1500 ft. I see the sign for Mineral Mt, 3351ft. The old turkey is silent now. Except for the sounds of him jerking off with his right hand. I'm happy to leave him to it. We're still climbing to get to Bylas, climbing through a truly spectacular canyon with high red buttes, and the sweeping shadows of birds of prey overhead that swoop out of the sun. My ears pop with the altitude. Signs say Gila County, San Carlos Indian Reservation. The guy's making some kind of funny noise, the way they all do, just before. There's nothing to see out the window but scrub and cactus and desert. The road looks almost black between two halves of desert and wobbles from side to side in the heat-haze. Nothing lives out here but snakes and coyotes and evil. I should be scared, but I aint.

'We got us a deal, honey,' he says, at last, as we flash through a dead-looking shack-town called Fort Thomas. He fetches up to the red paper pack tucked under the sunshield and offers me a cigarette with his right hand. 'When we git to Safford ya gonna let me take you in back?

'Maybe... keep your eyes on the road.'

'Ah surely will. Don't wanna overturn this baby. Not out here. Out here...' he says, 'out here they aint nobody to see, aint nobody...?'

He looks at me and there's something changed about him, nastier. I know what's going around his tiny mind. What's more, I guess he knows I know.

'Now don't be sore. A babe like you – it ain't nothin to you, but for a guy like me, why you're a dream – a sexy dream – you got it all, honey, those legs, why – you got me plain all worked up.'

'I heard you jackin' off,' I say, as if I'm pissed off. He doesn't speak. In the distance some dark shapes turn out to be, as we get closer, a kind of broken-down shack where some rough-looking guys are fixing up beat-up car hulks. I see a trailer behind the shack and a dog tied to the axle as we thunder past. Where's that dog gonna go? Run off? Like, where? One of the guys waves an oil rag and the driver waves back. There's a sign, too: Pima ½ mile.

'Good old boys,' he says and then as if to himself; 'wonder if they seen ya?'

'What's it to you?'

He laughs. There's a nasty edge to it. 'We could have had ourselves a party.'

'I know the kind of party you mean'.

A little further on we see a sign way up on the open horizon, standing alone and it don't even give a shadow on the road. It reads Safford & 666, 4 miles.

'I guess this is near enough,' he says, reaching for his gearstick. 'We don't wanna get us too near.'

'You better get me to Safford. I ain't walking, not in this heat.'

'You're okay with me, baby. And that's the truth.' He swerves the rig off the road and heads off into the dust clouds somewhere, working the gearstick and slowing us down as we roll over loose sand. I can taste the dust even though the windows are tight shut and the air conditioning's going full blast. The tanker judders to a bumpy halt and makes clicking and whirring noises, deflating, winding down. The dust settles all around, there's a thick film of it on the windows. The driver unbuckles the leather belt on his jeans. 'Safford's right over there,' he says.

'I can't see nothing.'

'Come over here, baby', he says quietly. 'Ahm gonna give you it but good. Ain't never had me one like you afore'.

'I don't want to get in no mess, mister,' I say. 'Don't want no oil on my teeshirt.'

'Take it off, honey. Or ah could tear it off...'

He comes lunging at me. I push his arms away. 'This ain't gonna work. You get in back, I'll take ma top off when you're ready.' I take off my shades an give him an encouraging smile.

'Yes ma'am!' he says eager to oblige. No idea of what's coming, like all of them. He sits on the edge of the bunk and yanks down his jeans. I can smell his sweat and the come that's drying on him.

'Lie back – or I ain't comin' over,' I say. And I pull the holdall over to me as I lift up the teeshirt and let him see. He lies back, goggling and gulping like he aint never saw a black pair and I pull the top over my head and lean over him and let him feel me, his rough hands grabbing and squeezing. I remember it, it reminds me... but my left hand is fumbling in the outer zip-pocket of the holdall.

'You're going to enjoy this, daddy, just like you done before,' I say, looking him in the eye, as my fingers locate the slim aluminium handle of the Swann & Morton 34, surgical scalpel, all ready in its tinfoil sleeve. 'Lie back – go on now, let me make you nice and big...'

The old guy's all meek now he has his pants down. 'Aw... hon – but, hey, I ain't near old enough to be your daddy. Shit, ya got that wrong...'

I'm in charge. He's lying flat, he's enjoying it, the fine line my fingernail is drawing around the base of his erect cock. Only it ain't my fingernail. He's still enjoying it when it scooshes out of him and makes a black arc in the air, splatters onto my breasts. The look of amazement when he guesses what ahm doin, the half-rise... *honey*! Ah got the power in me. Lordy. Past the moment of recovery, for first time he sees what ah done. He's too weak to get up, he gasps and gurgles like in films and there's red wet everywhere, on the bunk, the floor, the cab roof, even on them pin-ups. The bastard is in two pieces now, the old dead piece and the live pink bit that I'm squeezing in my hand. I feel burning hot, dia-bol-ically alive and all my childhood thoughts... I'm choking and trembling, and truth to tell, being sick all over...

Later, slowly and gradually, I begin to feel and hear and smell. The wet parts of me are cold in the air conditioning. I can hear my body working, responding in the complete silence of inner peace and all. Sadly, achingly, I gotta give it up, I guess. Let it go, climb down into the cruel heat of the burning desert that straightway begins to boil the fresh blood on my skin. There's silence at the zenith and nadir, and lowest point, the brink, the verge of death in life and there's like, buzzards, I guess, circling above only ah can't see none. I pull down the holdall, and check to see if there's blood on it. I wipe off blood spots with oil rag. I leave the holdall down by the wheel hub and walk a few yards, then throw myself in clean burning sand like I been wanting to do so long, and roll over and over, swimming in the ecstatic heat of it, abandoning myself to the friction, letting my legs flop and arms go loose, letting it fill my hair, absorb the blood off my skin an lie there spreadeagled, fully satisfied, relieved maybe a little, until it begins to hurt; the sun dazzle. I gotta get ma shades.

That's the beauty of pvc. Like skin, wipes clean easy and leaves no memories. Always looks shiny black, sexy like the road itself in the distance. I lug the holdall onto my shoulder and I walk lightly to the highway, ma feet burnin through my dainty lady shoes. I hate who I am but I can't see a way to stop. It's the only way I can feel real, can touch without fear. I need the precious moments of control to make up for all the power I lost, all the control that was used on me. I don't think about it anymore. I am numb to it. I know it will stop somehow sometime. But until then, I go on like the road. And in the distance I hear the humming of my daddy high behind the wheel of the next leviathan and the excitement begins to start all over again.

Hobbies in Retirement

Elissa Soave

It appeared that Laurence was not cut out for retirement, despite there being clear benefits to the state of enforced leisure that even he could admit to. For example, he did not miss the 07:20 from Surbiton to Waterloo, with its undignified scuffling around for a seat with his fellow professionals. Nor did he miss the unspoken manoeuvring and manipulating that took place in the academic cesspit in which he operated for almost 40 years. Nor still was he despondent at the lack of well-tended resentment that was the daily fare of his colleagues when another of their number published their findings in a top journal, or were featured in a fleeting slot on News at Ten, should their lifelong obsession happen to coincide with the hot topic of the day. No, it was fair to say that retirement offered him freedom from all of those things. And yet. In general, Laurence could not shake the feeling that the glass of later life was not so much half empty as smashed into crystal shards. Which were then stepped on by Laurence. In his bare feet.

Although it was now 25 years since he'd married Alice, he still remembered how impressed he'd been with the originality of her take on images of the labouring male body in Victorian paintings. That, and the way the soft, grey cashmere sheathed her 22-year-old breasts. She had been equally in thrall to his middle-aged charms, but then, all of Laurence's students had fancied him, how could they not – in his 40s, he'd been a force of nature, the centre of a personality cult that would have made Stalin blush. However, Laurence had recently become aware that his wife was seeing someone else. Possibly for some time, now that he thought about it.

For instance. On book club night, as he padded into the bedroom in search of his slippers, with his *Telegraph* crossword in one hand, and a glass of Jamiesons in the other, he caught her smoothing down the skirt of a frothy little outfit, turning sideways to the mirror to admire the turn of her ankle in open-toed sandals made of pink suede.

'You look nice', he said, though he was not given to compliments, especially addressed to his wife.

She patted her dress in a 'this old thing' gesture though it clearly was not old or insignificant at all since, for the last 15 or so years, she generally wore Sainsbury's one-size-fits-all jeans and one of a vast selection of shapeless long-sleeved tops. Laurence noticed later that she had left her copy of *The Master* on the table by her side of the bed.

For instance. Although he normally left all the finances to her, he happened to be checking through their transactions for a refund from British Gas, and he spotted the cost of an overnight stay at Hilton Islington from the previous month. Laurence had never been to the Hilton in Islington, though he believed it was one of their finest and served excellent breakfasts.

For instance. Laurence could not remember the last time his lounge pants from Next (medium, navy) had spent any time entwined on the bedroom carpet with her M&S nightdress (size 14, floral). Christ, he could remember a time when they would crawl all over each other every afternoon in his office, and night after night in his top-floor flat, and it was never enough. Backs arching, mouths seeking, limbs meshing, over and over, daily routine obscured by a thin film of sweat and longing, and they just couldn't get enough. Now, he couldn't even remember the last time he had seen his wife naked.

For instance. One Tuesday, he'd come home early from the golf club and even though he was three glasses of Merlot down, he was certain that he had seen the back end of their ex-neighbour, Jackson, jumping the fence with his tie swinging behind him and his hair looking distinctly unkempt. Even allowing for the fact that Laurence generally looked on the black side, there did not seem to be any possible positive spin to put on this. Except perhaps that Jackson was looking very youthful. Good for him.

Retirement had started so well for Laurence – epicurean picnics with Alice in Green Park, balmy evening strolls along the South Bank, marvelling at the street performers and enjoying double espressos by the river. And of course, lazy trips round the National, during which they reawakened their shared love for Titian and Constable. They even made it to the Tate Modern, raising their eyebrows at exhibitions embracing mass media and changing technologies, congratulating themselves on their ability to appreciate it all.

But after the tourist attractions of the city they'd called home for the last 25 years, what next? Somehow, coffee and cake tasted better when it was scarfed down between a departmental meeting with the Principal, and a tutorial with a hot, young first year. But when coffee was the highlight of the day, it just felt sad. In their slacks and crocs, he and Alice sat in silence on the same side of a table at Costa, and watched other people rushing in and ordering macchiato to take away, checking their watches and answering emails on their iPhones. For those people it was a coffee break in the middle of the day's business; for Laurence and Alice, the hot drink and stodge constituted the business of the day.

Perhaps that was why they'd started drinking so heavily. Laurence couldn't remember when it had become OK to pour a martini at 11, sip a couple of white wines at lunch then doze off with a port in front of Countdown. But he did know it was now entirely normal for both of them to squint at the final conundrum through a haze of liquor and the half-light of a dead afternoon.

After another lingering week of such afternoons, Alice declared she'd had enough and was going to join a book club. She'd met Jackson at Waitrose and he was looking remarkably well, considering. Jackson had assured her he was getting over Megan's shock departure with her Reiki master and really, meals for one from Waitrose's finest range were not that bad. Also, for the first time in his life he was able to do what he wanted to do, what he really wanted to do, not what Megan had chosen for him. And although he definitely had a novel in him, he'd decided to join a book club first and read what others had written. Laurence could picture Jackson leaning into Alice's trolley, treating her to a whiff of his English Leather cologne. 'We write in the shadows of every book we've ever read Alice', he'd have told her, or some such twaddle.

Every Tuesday thereafter she headed out to book club. Sometimes if there was an especially complex book under review, she'd have to go on a Thursday as well. Lately, it was not unknown for her to go along on a Friday night too, and last month, there had even been an overnight retreat. Colm Toibin was a writer of unimaginable depth, it seemed.

Despite his habitual gloom, Laurence had taken the bull by the horns and he too had taken up a hobby. He had enrolled in an evening course in electronics and electrical engineering. It was some way removed from his own field of Art History but Laurence found the lectures on installation procedures and wiring techniques fascinating. It was amazing what could be done with a length of electric wire and some fuses, it really was.

He set the whole thing up over a number of weeks on the nights Alice was at book club. He made sure the electric cable which led from the fuse box to the extractor fan hood above the cooker was not insulated and also that it was embedded only 10mm deep in the wall instead of the recommended 50mm. The cable meandered across the wall instead of running in strict horizontal or vertical lines, and finally he installed a stainless steel rack for the cooking implements sufficiently close to the cables so that one of the screws holding the rack to the wall was touching the live wire in the cable. A job of some beauty and precision, one might say a work of art.

When Alice got home that night, she was surprised to see the table set for two, with the Christmas tablecloth and even a scented candle.

'What's that disgusting old lady smell?' she said as she came into the room. The candle was scented with pot pourri, possibly not the best choice but still, Laurence thought the flickering light and the dreamy shadows it cast on the artex were very romantic.

'I thought we'd have a nice steak dinner, just the two of us', Laurence said.

'It's always just the two of us. I'm still doing the cooking, I take it?' Alice said as she took off her coat.

Laurence nodded and blew a low whistle as he took in her wide necked blouse and pencil skirt. Alice ignored him and moved to the cooker. She poured some oil into the pan and turned the knob of the back ring as she reached up for the spatula.

'Jackson at book club tonight was he?' asked Laurence casually, not looking at Alice.

Alice's arm fell back to her side and she spun round to face Laurence, her cheeks flushing slightly.

'I'm sure I didn't notice. Why do you ask?'

'Oh, no reason', said Laurence, his eyes fixed on the kitchen utensils hanging enticingly on the rack.

Alice smoothed her skirt and turned back to the cooker. Her right hand approached the spatula; Laurence held his breath and his eyes widened.

'You know, if you've got something to say, please do just say it, Laurence', said Alice, turning back to her husband.

'No, no, nothing at all. I'm looking forward to my steak, aren't you, darling?' he said looking at the hot oil, now spitting and hissing in the pan.

'You should take up a hobby, it'd do you the world of good', said Alice, moving away from the cooker, and taking a half-empty bottle of Chablis out of the fridge.

'Yes, indeed. Ah, the steaks...?' said Laurence, beads of perspiration standing out on his brow.

Alice gave her husband a quizzical look as she poured herself a glass of chilled, white wine. 'Are you alright Laurence? You seem... edgy.'

'Nothing a good steak wouldn't put right', said Laurence testily, gesturing towards the cooker with two chubby fingers.

Alice took a sip from her glass then returned to the cooker and stretched her hand towards the rack of utensils.

'You know, Laurence...'

Laurence was surprised at the speed with which the electric current passed through the cables and into her body, causing her to fizzle and tremble. He watched with some interest as her hair rose and fluffed outwards, making her look like a blushing porcupine. After a few seconds, he had to put his hand over his nose so that he could not smell the hideous odour of burning follicles and scorched skin.

When it was over, Laurence felt a wave of fresh optimism wash over him. He was only 68 after all, and perhaps now was the time to write that book he'd never had time to contemplate when he was working. He thought maybe a monograph on Hogarth's Marriage a la Mode or something on those lines, rather than pure fiction. He might even make a start after his steak.

The Baron's Basement

Shona MacLean

When the bodies were discovered, it soon became clear that it had all been the fault of Hugh MacDiarmid, as things often are. Before proceeding further, though, an explanation of the Baron Taylor's Bookshop might be useful, for those unfamiliar with that establishment.

The Crime Fiction department of that bookshop is to be found in the basement - on account of Miss Dalrymple, spinster and only child of Mr Aeneas Dalrymple (founder of the Baron's in 1932) and, from her father's death in 1951 until her own in 1992, proprietor of the business.

Georgina could *almost* remember Miss Dalrymple. She had been barely five years old when the grave, black-bordered notice had appeared on the glass-panelled front door of the Baron's, regretfully intimating the sad news of the proprietor's passing, that the funeral would be private, and the shop closed for the coming week. 'Oh Dear,' her mother had said, as they had been confronted by it on their regular Saturday morning visit to town, 'we'll have to go to John Menzies instead.'

Georgina had not complained, but as her mother well knew, a visit to John Menzies was not at all the same thing as a visit to the Baron's. John Menzies might well have a stand of brightly coloured magazines near the front door, and a sweets section by the till, but that was neither here nor there to Georgina. Her own copy of *The Twinkle* was delivered on a Tuesday afternoon, and she and her mother always bought their sweets in Woolworths. Neither was it of any interest to Georgina that John Menzies stocked CDs and tapes in its music department, in the basement. Georgina's teenaged cousin David was known to spend most of his daytime hours haunting the place, but as far as Georgina was concerned, it was a waste of a good basement.

Basements, Georgina had come to learn, were places for murderers to lurk and their victims to be ingeniously done away with (she was vague about the details, her mother being disappointingly reticent on such matters). Each Saturday, after Georgina had made her own selection from the children's department of the Baron's, she and her mother would descend together to the basement, by a narrow and somewhat rickety stairs to the Crime Fiction department. It had never occurred to Georgina to wonder why this particular department should be found in so inaccessible a place. It seemed to her just the right sort of place for the books she knew were stocked there, and those not prepared to risk the stairs and the poor lighting would be well-advised to stay away from such material in any case.

In this, Georgina's reasoning was not so very far away from that of Miss Dalrymple herself, who had decreed on her father's death that works of crime fiction should be removed from their location by the front door and placed in the basement, on account of her view that stories of murder, and *worse*, were 'not quite nice'. Miss Dalrymple would have preferred not to stock any crime fiction at all, but a not inconsiderable financial acumen had made clear to her that the reading public was full of degenerates prepared to pay hard cash to indulge their depravities. Tales of 'True Crime' she utterly refused to stock, responding to any who asked that she believed they might find it on the shelves of the railway station newsagents, along with other books for people who did not read books.

There were, periodically, complaints from visiting Americans and some of the Baron's regular clientele about the inaccessibility of the Crime Fiction section. To the locals, many of whom Miss Dalrymple had known since her days of assiduous study at Inverness Royal Academy, she would respond that they could hardly be in requirement of further insight into the darker side of life; the Americans she simply claimed not to be able to understand.

It was over ten years after the passing of Miss Dalrymple that Georgina, her heart pounding in exultation, had finally entered the Baron's by the back door, at precisely 8 a.m. on the first morning of her employment as 'the Saturday girl'. By this time, sadly, there were no Dalrymples at the helm of the Baron's, but Miss Dalrymple had presciently left her shop to the two sons of a cousin whom she knew for a certainty to have no interest in books. The young men's delight at being left such a lucrative legacy had been short-lived: under the full terms of their second-cousin's will, the shop must not be put up for sale for at least twenty years and matters pertaining to the buying *and display* of the books were to be approved by Mr Gavin Dinwoodie, trusted employee of long-standing; further... and there were many further provisions, so many in fact, that the men eventually threw up their hands and conceded almost all to Mr Dinwoodie. They did, however, out of spite, insert small irritants of interference into their dealings with the Baron's. One instance of which being their insistence on Mr Dinwoodie adopting the title of 'Manager'. Mr Dinwoodie did not at all like the indignity thus thrust upon him, still less the accompanying plastic badge they insisted he wear – he himself had begun his career in the Baron's as a Saturday boy not long after the last bloom of youth had finally departed Miss Dalrymple's cheeks. For ten years, Mr Dinwoodie dutifully pinned on the loathsome badge with an air of quiet despondency heart-breaking to all who knew and loved the Baron's. But then had come the day, almost a year in to her employment as the Saturday girl, that Georgina had tentatively, aware that it might be a sackable offence, presented to him a small gift, a brass badge, with the legend 'Mr G. Dinwoodie - Head Bookseller', engraved upon it. She quietly suggested that the other, less pleasing plastic item could be kept in the drawer beneath the counter, for use only should the nephews unexpectedly appear. Mr Dinwoodie had murmured his thanks, and carefully affixed the gift to his jumper. Georgina had not known it, but from that day on, the Baron's was hers.

Twenty years to the day of Miss Dalrymple's death, the letter from the solicitor arrived. The Baron's was to be sold, as a business opportunity or a going concern, the now middle-aged brothers cared not which, and the 'Manager' was instructed to make all ready for putting the place on the market. Georgina, now graduated in English Literature, had returned to the Baron's as assistant bookseller. After reading the letter aloud, Mr Dinwoodie had coughed and said, 'Miss Stewart, the back room if you would be so good.'

Mr Dinwoodie placed the letter on his desk, securing it beneath a brass bust of Walter Scott, whose nose Georgina had always thought off, somehow. Mr Dinwoodie smiled. 'I think, Miss Stewart, you know the Baron's almost as well as I do myself, and have its interests very much in your heart.'

Georgina had blushed.

Mr Dinwoodie continued, 'That is why I think you should buy the Baron's.'

Never before had Georgina suspected Mr Dinwoodie of senility, but she now wondered whether the shock of the solicitor's letter had proved too much.

'But Mr Dinwoodie…' she began.

He raised a benign eyebrow in interruption. 'You are about to protest that you are too young, and that you do not have the funds. Though youthful, you are not too young, and you have an old soul. As to the funds, you may not have them, but I do. Over sixty years of continuous employment and the prescient purchase of my small flat across the river many years ago have allowed me to build up not insubstantial savings.'

'But then, Mr Dinwoodie, surely you should…'

The other eyebrow. 'Buy it myself? No, Miss Stewart, while you are not too young, I am most certainly too old. Besides, I fancy sometimes I can still smell the Virginia of Mr Dalrymple's pipe, hear the tread of Miss Dalrymple's foot upon the stair. It is not for me to be the owner of the Baron's. I have been its guardian these last twenty years, but now I am tired. I feel a reasonable though not excessive offer would be acceptable to the young gentlemen, and we should certainly not need a bank loan. Are you game, my dear?'

Mr Dinwoodie made it plain that he wished to remain an employee of the Baron's for as long as he could be of use, and that the money, once handed over, the book shop was Georgina's to do with as she pleased. He was confident, he said following a small cough, that she would honour the spirit of the place, but he fully realised that a young person would wish to modernise the establishment, and that with the behemoths of the book chains, the supermarkets and the almost unmentionable on-line selling of books, there was a fight to be had. Miss Stewart would not find him standing in her way as she carried that fight to the foe. 'But he did very much hope, that certain things, in deference to the late Miss Dalrymple …'

Georgina had nodded tactfully. 'The Crime Fiction department,' she said.

'Just so,' said Mr Dinwoodie.

'In the basement it will most certainly stay,' said Georgina.

Thus ensued four happy years of progress and change for the Baron's. A bank loan was required for the conversion of the unused top floor to a coffee shop. Mr Dinwoodie had not demurred, but for eighteen months after the instalment of the Italian espresso machine he had continued to carry his green tartan flask of tea to work with him and to drink from it in the back room, at rigidly adhered to tea-break times that had not changed in sixty years. Only the lure of a treacle scone finally enticed him to the top floor, although the espresso machine was never called in to use on his behalf.

Occasionally, they would host visiting authors. Mr Dinwoodie himself purchased the wine for these events, and seemed rather to enjoy them, although, in deference to the feelings of Miss Dalrymple, there were certain proponents of *tartan noir* whose evenings he felt unable to attend.

There was no cloud on the horizon, until that sunny Friday morning when, Georgina having disabled the alarm and entered the shop, she had begun to make her rounds of its departments. All was well in the coffee shop, children's section, and in poetry and drama, however a minor disruption in Scottish literature had seen the Kelmans and the Alexander McCall Smiths get mixed up again.

And so to crime, accessible by a recently installed lift, although Georgina always took the stairs herself. And that was when she found the bodies.

The screws of a shelf, in the rather cramped and awkward-of-access space beneath the stairs had been worked loose by the rattling of the lift, and the shelf had finally come away, taking some plasterboard with it. It was through the resultant hole in the plaster that Georgina first glimpsed that bony hand. Crouching, she gave the plaster a tentative tug, thereby dislodging a second shelf. Peering through the now substantial gap, her attention was immediately taken by the book still gripped in the skeleton's right hand. It was a first edition, Ian Rankin's *Wolfman*. Georgina shivered: they'd changed the title to *Tooth and Nail*, but the book had been called *Wolfman* when first it had come out, in 1992.

Only then did she peer a little further in to the space behind, a long bricked up cellar. There lay a second skeleton, its well - made but unpleasantly decayed tweed suit, only confirming what she already suspected. The hole where the man's skull had clearly been smashed called to mind something else.

In another establishment, a person coming upon such a gruesome find would immediately have telephoned to the police. But this was the Baron's, and Georgina had read enough detective stories to know that that was unlikely to expedite matters, and certainly would not bring them to a satisfactory conclusion. After replacing what she could of the fallen plasterboard, and concealing it behind some particularly heavy and uninteresting hardbacks, she removed the light bulb from the under-stair alcove, and went up to await the arrival of Mr Dinwoodie.

She was in the coffee-shop, half way down a large flat white and checking some details in the Josephine Tey biography she had brought up from the ground floor display, when she heard the staff door at the back open then close again at precisely one minute to eight, as it had been doing for more than sixty-five years now. After a moment she called down, 'Do you think we might have a word, Mr Dinwoodie?'

When he was seated across from her she began. 'I have been down in the Crime

Department this morning, making my checks.'

He nodded approvingly.

'I noticed,' she hesitated, 'that some of the under stair plasterwork and shelving had come loose, on account of the lift, I imagine.'

'The most likely cause,' agreed Mr Dinwoodie, watching her.

'I found, on closer inspection, a copy of Ian Rankin's *Wolfman*, along with some other – things.'

'Ah,' said Mr Dinwoodie. 'I rather hoped I might have passed on before those things were discovered.'

There was a pause.

'Did Miss Dalrymple always dislike crime fiction?' Georgina asked at last.

'Why, no!' he said, his eyes brightening. 'As a young woman, she had been inordinately fond of it, as was her father. Those were golden days of the craft, and Miss Dalrymple devoured her favourites with glee: tales of Miss Marple and Monsieur Poirot, Lord Peter Wimsey, Mr Campion, Inspector Grant...' here, his voice trailed off, and he glanced sadly at the biography across the table form him.

'Was Inspector Grant a particular favourite?' enquired Georgina.

'Miss Dalrymple adored the works of Miss Tey, until, that was, the day Mr MacDiarmid came in to the shop.'

'Mr MacDiarmid? Hugh MacDiarmid?'

'Yes, he had been visiting Mr Neil Gunn. It was the time of the Gaelic mod, and the two gentlemen came in in the afternoon, mornings being more difficult on account of the Whisky drinking that attends such cultural events. As you will know,' – Georgina had not known – 'Mr MacDiarmid was a passionate admirer of crime literature, and naturally soon fell into discussion with Miss Dalrymple about their favourites. It was when I saw Miss Dalrymple's face turn ashen that I realised something had gone terribly wrong. She was never a woman of high colour, you understand, but she was seldom ashen. The conversation had turned to the Inspector Grant novels of Josephine Tey, and Mr MacDiarmid had been astonished to learn that Miss Dalrymple did not realise Josephine Tey was the pseudonym of Miss Elizabeth MacKintosh, fruiterer's daughter, of Castle Street.'

Beth MacKintosh. And not three minute's walk from the Baron's Bookshop. 'They must have gone to school together,' said Georgina.

'Indeed they had,' affirmed Mr Dinwoodie glumly. 'Inverness Royal Academy. And that was where the breach began. There had been an incident on the hockey field, apparently, for which Miss Dalrymple had been very publicly chastised, although she always maintained that the fault had been Beth Mackintosh's. And later in the same year it was Miss Mackintosh, and not Miss Dalrymple, who was awarded the music prize for which Miss Dalrymple had so assiduously practised. She never sat at the piano again, and it goes without saying that, on learning the true identity of Josephine Tey, she vowed never to read another work of crime fiction.'

'And how did her father take this?' Georgina prompted gently.

'Ah,' Mr Dinwoodie sighed and studied the table top. 'Badly. It had been one of their shared pleasures, and that companionship was denied the old gentleman. She went so far, eventually, as to declare that when she was in charge of the Baron's, *no* crime fiction would be stocked. It was very soon afterwards that one evening, at the close of business, Mr Dalrymple put on his hat and intimated his intention of visiting his solicitor.'

A horrible dread began to creep over Georgina. 'The nephew,' she barely whispered.

'The nephew,' affirmed Mr Dinwoodie gravely. 'When I arrived the next morning, I was surprised by Mr Dalrymple's hat, which looked to have rolled through the doorway from the back room and come to rest on the shop floor. I took a firm hold of my umbrella and approached the door. You cannot imagine the horror that greeted me. Mr Dalrymple was sprawled on his back, surrounded by blood which had clearly poured from a large gash on his head. Beside him lay the bust of Sir Walter Scott, which has never quite recovered, and slumped in the corner, sobbing uncontrollably was Miss Dalrymple. Her father had informed her he intended to leave her well-provided for, but to bequeath the Baron's to his nephew. He would be scarcely cold in his grave, he had said, before the works of Christie, Sayers, Tey *et al*. were thrown in after him. In the heat of the moment, she had picked up the first thing that came to hand – the bust – and struck him with it. She had then spent a grief-stricken night with the corpse, waiting for me to arrive, for she knew I would not fail her.'

'And you didn't,' said Georgina gently.

'I have the deepest respect for the law, and adhere to it whenever proper, but to have reported Miss Dalrymple's act to the authorities would have helped no-one, and it would have been the end of the Baron's. I put a death notice on the door, intimated that the funeral was to be private at Mr Dalrymple's own request, and assisted that poor lady in moving her father's body to the cellar in the basement. By the time the shop re-opened a week later, the Crime Fiction had been moved to its new home, and life returned more or less to normal.'

'Until *Wolfman*.'

'Yes,' conceded Mr Dinwoodie. 'On the day that that particular book arrived, Miss Dalrymple insisted on supervising the deliveries herself. Although ninety-six, she remained a person of great stamina. It was a great relief to my assistant, Miss Macpherson, when she picked up a copy of *Wolfman* and declared her intention to pursue the study of natural history. Poor Miss Macpherson was by that time "almost worn to a frazzle with her", as she later confessed, which was why she had not realised that an Ian Rankin book was hardly the thing for Miss Dalrymple. I do not say, of course, that Mr Rankin is the worst, far from it, but still you will see the problem?'

Georgina did.

'It was only after the rest of the staff had left that I realised I had not seen Miss Dalrymple for some time. On entering the back room, I immediately realised that all was not well. There was a look in Miss Dalrymple's eye that 'manic' does not do justice to, and her *coiffure* was markedly dishevelled. She held the book out towards me. "You didn't tell me," and said, laughing quite unpleasantly.'

"'Did not tell you what, Miss Dalrymple?" I asked.'

"'That the world of Inspector Alan Grant is no more !" And with an agility I could not have guessed at, she was round the desk and past me before I had recovered myself. By the time I got to the door, she had reached the top of the stairway to the crime department. I watched, horrified, as she charged downwards without even switching on the light. The stumble, thumps and final crack were horrible to hear. I found her with her head at a dreadful angle, the book still clutched in her hand and her neck quite broken.'

Georgina saw it all as clearly as if she herself had been there. 'But why did you not telephone the police?'

'I considered it,' he said. 'Indeed, the receiver was in my hand when I stopped. I do not believe the police to be as inept as they are often portrayed, and I feared that if they began to examine the basement they might come upon – *other things*. That would have done poor Miss Dalrymple no good, to say nothing of what would have become of the reputation of the Baron's. I hope you understand, Miss Stewart.'

'I understand completely, Mr Dinwoodie.'

She glanced at her watch, and he at the clock. 'It is 8:30, Miss Stewart.'

'Of course,' she said. 'I am sorry to have kept you. But if you are free at all this evening?'

'I have no engagements Miss Stewart.'

'Then I would be obliged if you would stay behind after the shop closes and help me with some shelving matters in the Crime Department.'

The Moth

Chris McQueer

Being a moth, I am driven by an insatiable desire to fly into a human being's ear canal, burrow through the soft tissue and bone inside and take control of their brain. I will then live undetected as a human for around eighty years. The host's friends and family will have no idea their loved one, a person they may have known their entire life, is actually being operated from within by a humble house moth.

However, only a small number of moths in recorded history have achieved this. I am confident I can join their ranks. I have spent weeks studying my chosen host. He is a very large, very strong behemoth of a man with a penchant for alcohol. Fond of getting extremely inebriated, almost to the point of unconsciousness and with fat, stumpy fingers that will barely fit in his ear, he shouldn't put up too much of a fight as I eat my way into his mind.

Today is the day I will finally make my move. Big Gordon, as his equally alcohol obsessed friends call him, has been getting as drunk as humanly possible out in the baking hot sun all day and he is due to collapse at any moment. I will leave him to enter a deep sleep, then, when I am satisfied he no longer possesses the dexterity to stop me, I will fly into his left ear.

I am clinging to the wall of what is soon to be my new home. Camouflaged against the exposed brick work, I am invisible to the flock of pigeons pecking around the garden. I watch Big Gordon rise from his sun lounger, his sudden movement thankfully scaring away the winged vermin that like to prey upon my species.

The delicate human skin on his face has been beaten red raw by the sun. It looks painful and I am not particularly looking forward to dealing with the sensation of the skin peeling from my nice new face. He lumbers forward a few steps before stopping and swaying side to side with such grace and elegance I am practically hypnotised by his movements. He rocks backwards and forwards on his feet then falls face first with a dull thud into the grass. He has surely broken his nose but he shows no sign of being in any pain. I am also not looking forward to having to inhale fetid odours up through my new (possibly broken) proboscis rather than just sensing them using my antennae.

Watching this creature put his body through so much punishment, I can't help but feel I am doing him a favour by taking control. It won't be long until he is out of his misery.

With the pigeons having fled in terror and my host safely rendered unconscious by his fall, it is time to fulfil my plan. I swoop down from my vantage point and land on Big Gordon's soft, fleshy cheek. All he will feel, if anything, is the soft flutter of my wings and a gentle tickling from feet.

Many moths favour the dive bomb technique; hurtling into their chosen host's ear at great speed with the aim of lodging themselves deep into the aural cavity. I have observed many moths using this technique and found this causes humans to panic and plunge their fingers in after them, mashing them to a pulp. A more delicate approach is required if you ask me.

I feel around the opening to his ear using my front legs. I am astounded by the the flowing curves of the cartilage and the ridges that appear almost like ripples on a lake. I tuck in my wings, streamlining myself to move through the canal. I am filled with a surge of adrenaline and the urge to charge in as fast and hard as I can is a difficult one to resist. I compose myself though. I have a long way to go.

I squeeze my head into the dark tunnel. Tiny, oily hairs tickle my soft underbelly as I slide along, not a totally unpleasant sensation. His snoring creates a deep, thunderous rumble and I can feel his entire head vibrating. Air rushes in and out underneath me. The warmth envelops me and the darkness sharpens my senses. A sharp metallic smell overloads my antennae. I flick my tongue out slowly, wincing in anticipation of the bitter taste of his ear wax. I suck up the foul matter as I continue to push my way along. The wax coats my entire body. My wings are slicked down with the greasy substance. A special gland in my mouth goes into overdrive as I swallow as much of the wax as I can, producing an acid which will be secreted from the end of tongue that will soften the bone of Big Gordon's skull, allowing me to dig my way into his brain.

But before I can think about the arduous task of digging through seven millimetres of solid bone, I have to burst through his ear drum. I caress the paper thin structure. I can feel its tautness straight away. I have to get through it quick or the scratching noise of my mandibles gnawing at it will awaken my sleeping host. I pierce the membrane and force my way through into his inner ear.

This is often where things go wrong for the few intrepid moths who make it this far. On the other side of the ear drum is what is known as the Eustachian tube, a deep chasm which leads to the mouth and to almost certain death. In order to prevent this fate occurring, you have to deftly manoeuvre your way around the edges of this pit. My chosen technique is to stick my feet into clumps of ear wax, giving me extra grip. By doing this you can edge your way around the abyss and latch on to the cochlea at the other side. This method was used by a house moth, like myself, who managed to successfully take a over a human being and become the world's foremost lepidopterist.

My host remains lying flat out on the ground, undisturbed by the goings on inside his head. I am very excited at the thought of the long rest I am going to enjoy when I fuse with his brain and take full control of him. I may sleep for a fortnight.

The cochlea is an especially strange organ in the human body, which in itself is essentially a big bag of strange organs. Comprised of a maze of delicate bony walls and filled with chambers of air and fluid, its purpose is, as yet, unknown to us moths. It is here I get to use my newly produced bone dissolving acid for the first time. I roll out my tongue and I can feel the hot, caustic liquid surging forward to the tip. It erupts in a furious jet which

I aim at the centre of the cochlea. The labyrinthine structure of this part of the human ear would prove difficult to traverse if I was smaller but as I am a somewhat rotund moth, I will be able to use my bulk to forge a path straight through to the skull.

I dissolve the brittle bone wall and a steady stream of fluid washes over me. I wait until the flow subsides before entering the first chamber. As my feet feel around the moist floor of the chamber, I pick up a soft vibration.

Big Gordon is waking up.

His normally deep voice has risen several octaves with fear. The cochlear liquid is rushing back in behind me. He is attempting to get to his feet. The hot sensation of the acid dissolving this delicate part of his ear must have put his body into panic mode. He will be fully awake in moments and will feel me wriggling through his head, causing him to panic further.

This is not good.

My host wants me out immediately. He is now upright. The brain is frantically sending signals to get Big Gordon to jam a finger into his ear. As he does this, the pressure forces me deeper into the cochlea. Human aural juice sloshes around. Acid is spraying forth from my tongue and I scratch at the membranes and bony walls with all of my might. My legs, laden with wax, prise apart the melting bone. I break through the cochlea and I am now at the skull.

I can feel Big Gordon slapping at his ear. A cacophony of sound fills my own head as he screams and forces any object he can find in after me. But I am well out of reach. The noise leaves me disorientated but I remain focused. Nothing can stop me now. I latch onto his skull. Some wax remains stuck my feet and I use this to keep attached to the smooth surface. I unfurl my tongue and concentrate the stream of acid on the one spot. It burns its way through, eroding the dense bone away. I feel the hole widening under my feet.

Deeper it goes.

Deeper.

Deeper.

Deeper.

I can feel the wrinkled surface of his brain.

I am in.

Big Gordon once again falls to the ground unconscious.

His mind absorbs me. Moths and humans are made to merge with one another. Our planet's two most intelligent species coming together to create a perfect hybrid being. Big Gordon's memories play out before me intertwined with my own. My superior consciousness submerges his and I take control.

Five Poems in Five Tongues

Aurelia Lassaque (Occitan)

Crimi

La tampa tustava
contra la paret,
era sola
al dedins de l'ostal
per velhar prèp del mòrt
dins sa cambra a ela.
Sola amb el
sa paur
e sos joguets
escampats pel sòl.
Se diguèt que lo velhariá
fins a l'alba
puèi que li fariá una tomba
amb un entarrament,
al lausèrt qu'aviá tuat.

Five Poems in Five Tongues

James Thomas (English)

Crime

The shutter clattered
against the wall;
she was alone
inside the house,
in her room keeping watch
over the dead body.
Alone with it,
her fear
and her toys
scattered on the floor.
She thought she'd guard it
until dawn
then she'd make a grave
in which to bury
the lizard she'd killed.

Five Poems in Five Tongues

Harry Giles (Orcadian)

Crime

The brods brattled
agin the waa;
sheu wis alone
ben the hoose
tae wauk the corp
in her reum.
Alone wi hid,
her dreid
an her gemms
skaeld ower the fluir.
Sheu thowt sheu'd wauk
til the gray
then mak a graff
an a beurin
fer this lisard sheu'd felled.

(the French & Shetlandic translations of this poem can be found at:
www.guttermag.co.uk/five_tongues)

Five Poems in Five Tongues

Aurelia Lassaque (Occitan & French)

Pantais

Fai freg dins mon anma
es romantic e desuet.
Ieu
auriái presa la nau en Grècia.
A Santorin auriái limpat
fins a la mar.
Auriái penjat mon lum
a la branca d'un olivièr
e dins un ostal blanc
auriái aimat de pescaires esperitals
e de monges desfrocats.

Fantasme

Il fait froid dans mon âme
c'est romantique et désuet.
Moi
j'aurais pris le bateau en Grèce.
A Santorin j'aurais glissé
jusqu'à la mer.
J'aurais pendu ma lampe
a la branche d'un olivier
et dans une maison blanche
j'aurais aimé des pécheurs spirituels
et des moines défroqués.

Five Poems in Five Tongues

Harry Giles (Orcadian)
and *Christie Williamson* (Shetlandic)

Fantasie

Hid's caald in me saal:
hou romantic an aald-farrant.
I
wad o taen the bott fae Greece.
At Santorini wad o davvid
oot tae sea.
Wad o hingid me lamp
on the brench o an olive
an in a white hoose
wad o lued seilie fishersinners
an defrockid freers.

Fantasy

Hit's cowld in mi sowl
hit's romantic an sweet.
Me
I'd a jumped on da boat in Greece.
At Santorini I'd a lowsed
fur da faur haaf.
I'd a dangled mi lamp
aff a olive tree branch
an in a whicht hoose
I'd a loved spiritual fishermen
an monks, defrocked.

(the English translation of this poem can be found at:
www.guttermag.co.uk/five_tongues)

Five Poems in Five Tongues

Aurelia Lassaque (Occitan)

A l'ora del solstici...

A l'ora del solstici
lo pòble vestit de fusta
atira dins sa rama
d'aucèls sens cara.

Lo riu barrutlaire
carreja dusca als ribals
sos remembres de nèu.

Los aubres de ma selva
an rogejat al primièr jorn de l'estieu.

Los òmes de la vila
an dich qu'aquò's la rovilha
e que ven del Japon.

Mas eles sabon pas
que los aubres d'aquela comba
dins lo secret de lors rasigas
alisan de pèiras vivas
que se mèton a somiar
que l'aura e la pluèja
las prendràn nusas sul bard
a l'ora del solstici.

Five Poems in Five Tongues

Christie Williamson (Shetlandic)

At da oor o da solstice

At da oor o da solstic
efokk riggit in wid
coort intae dir branches
birds wi nae faes.

Da rogue burn
haals tae da waves
hit's mindin o snaa.

Mi sylvan trees
has come red wi Johnsmas.

Da toonie
sis caain hit roost
blaan in fae Japan.

But dey dunna keen
at da trees in dis dale
in dir secret deep röts
fondle livin stons
at start dreamin
da wind an da rain
'll takk dem nekkit on da clay
at da oor o da solstice.

(the English, French & Orcadian- translations of this poem can be found at:
www.guttermag.co.uk/five_tongues)

Five Poems in Five Tongues

Aurelia Lassaque (French)
and *Harry Giles* (Orcadian)

Il a bu le lait de sa mère...

Il a bu le lait de sa mère,
mangé la chair de sa femme,
brûlé la cervelle de ses enfants
mais il ne comprend pas sa solitude.
Sa maison boit la pluie,
sa terre avale les pierres.
Il demeura le roi de l'histoire qu'il raconte
c'est le privilège des monstres d'ici-bas.

O his mither he swallaed the milk...

O his mither he swallaed the milk,
o his wumman he aet the maet,
o his bairns he brunt the braens
but he canno rackon his loneliness.
His hoose swallaes the raen,
his yird scaffs the staens.
He'll aye bide laird o his yarns,
fer that's the laa fer geyars doun here.

(the Occitan, English & Shetlandic translations of this poem can be found at:
www.guttermag.co.uk/five_tongues)

Five Poems in Five Tongues

Aurelia Lassaque (French & Occitan)

Le rêve d'Eurydice

Nous creuserons de nouveaux sillons que nous couvrirons de cendre.

Nous verrons mourir le vent qui charrie l'oubli.

J'aurai des pommes dans ma poche volées à plus pauvre que moi.

Nous les pèlerons avec des épées.

Et avec les restes de nos rêves

nous en bâtirons d'autres

par-delà les feux

et la frontière du regard.

Lo sòmi d'Euridícia

Cavarem d'autras regas que cobrirem de cendre.

Veirem morir lo vent carrejaire d'oblit.

Aurai de pomas dins ma pòcha raubadas a mai paure que ieu.

Las pelarem amb d'espasas.

E amb çò que sòbra de nòstres sòmis

ne bastirem mai

delà los fuòcs

e la termièra de l'agach.

(the English, Orcadian & Shetlandic translations of this poem can be found at:
www.guttermag.co.uk/five_tongues)

She knew very little English back then, and she'd learned more Doric than English since from the Fish Filleters who'd grown up in the town. They told stories all day long as their hands robotically sliced open each fish and howked out its guts.

Extract form the Novel *Quines at Sea*
Shane Strachan

Extract from the Novel *Quines at Sea*

Shane Strachan

Her name is Sylwia. She moved from Lublin to Fraserburgh at the beginning of 2008. Apart from the cold, she liked it at first: it was a lot quieter than her home city, and she could walk by the sea everyday. It was the only thing she still loved after all these years, watching the waves crash through the black rocks near the fish factory, and the daring surfers ride coorse waves in the middle of winter.

From the day she arrived, she'd been gutting fish at the same factory down by the beach. She knew very little English back then, and she'd learned more Doric than English since from the Fish Filleters who'd grown up in the town. They told stories all day long as their hands robotically sliced open each fish and howked out its guts. It took Sylwia months to get up to speed with them, and some months longer before she felt confident enough to join in their conversations and tell some of her own stories: of old, dusty Lublin; of her family back home who awaited the bank transfer of half her wage every month; of the friends she left behind who spoke to her on webcam late at night, who she begged to come join her in Scotland. But they wouldn't now that work was drying up and wages were beginning to stall. That's why things had turned so sour between the foreign workers and the ones from the Broch. That's why Sandra hated her.

Sylwia had known from day one that she was being paid far less than the workers native to the town. She couldn't complain – that's why they hired her, and the wage was still worth moving all these miles for, compared to the pittance she'd made in Poland. But one winter had been particularly bad out at sea and hardly any fish passed along the conveyer belt at work. All the gutters knew it, but none of them dared to say out loud that jobs would be on the line.

Sandra, their unofficial leader of sorts, just spoke of all the work that would come their way in summer: a stream of silver would flood through the factory and into their bank accounts.

Sandra had a lot less to say when she lost her job at the beginning of spring. She went straight from the manager's office ben to the processing line, her gutting knife in hand. She picked Sylwia out of the line of Polish, Lithuanian, Latvian and Bulgarian workers.

This is aa your fucking fault! She'd bawled, the tip of the knife pointing at Sylwia's face.

Fit you on aboot? Sylwia laughed, completely oblivious to what was happening.

Me and every other fucker that's spent half their life here has just lost their job because o you foreign tinks.

That's when Sandra had spat in Sylwia's face and a fight broke out. Sylwia was knocked over near the start and lay there until she saw Sandra being carried out of the factory by the manager and his brother, the depute manager.

The stream of abuse she received in town got worse from then on. She couldn't leave her door without someone shouting something at her about being Polish, Eastern European, foreign, a job thief, a prostitute, a junkie...

She soon took to staying indoors most of the time, only venturing out for work, or to the shops when her flatmate would brave the outside world with her.

And the worst o it is... she said to Charlene as they sat on the wooden floor by the bunk she'd lain in. The worst o it is, that I had to listen as aabdy moan about not being able to get NHS dentist, and in my home country, all this time, I am trainee dentist. I was saving up my money to study it here, but that dream has gone. Aathing starts costing owre much and I have nae money even to send hame. So I think I hae to go back to Poland, and that's fan I hear aboot you quines in factory, aboot you gan oot to sea. Folk say to me that Sandra is telling aabdy in the pub that you're gan to Amsterdam. I think, perfect! I will get hame fae there easy. So I sneaked on boat night afore you leave harbour. Door was unlocked – too easy.

Trust Sandra! Charlene whined.

Aye, she's a bitch, eh? Sylwia started laughing. Charlene would have laughed as well, if it weren't for the realisation that Sylwia looked so pale and thin as she laughed.

Have you really been hiding doon there for two hale days?

Oh yes. I try bide in ice room and it's affa caul. I move through to boiler room and, even with earmuffs on my heid, the whole world shaks aroond me. I hivna slept till just noo.

And you ate some melon fae the fridge? Charlene asked. She fumbled around in her pocket until she felt the strand of hair wrap round her finger. She pulled it out and showed it to Sylwia.

Bloody hell, you are Sherlock Holmes.

No, I just hate hairs in ma food, Charlene said. Spikking o food, I think it's aboot time you got a proper feed. I think ma mam's makin spaghetti Bolognese.

I canna go up the stair. I canna be near her, Sylwia whimpered.

I winna let her lay a finger on ye, Charlene said standing up. Come on, ye'r wasting awa to nithing. Charlene helped pull Sylwia up onto her feet and they made their way up through the hatch.

Sylwia hid behind her as they neared the dining table. All of the quines were sat round it, a pot of Bolognese and a pot of spaghetti sat in front of them.

Right, I'm afraid ye'r aa gan to have to budge up to mak room for me and our new crewmate.

You have got to be joking me, Sandra said, her spoon held up in the air.

Fit ye gan to dee wie that Sandra? Howk oot the peer quine's een?

Sandra returned to eating, her bottom lip heavy. Charlene and Sylwia sat down at the end of the table.

Now, dinna dare tell me ye dinna like spaghetti or I *will* hae to chuck ye owreboard.

I've been eating frozen chips past two days. Onything is better than frozen chips that are still fucking frozen.

All the quines except Sandra burst out laughing.

It wasn't long before the pots in the middle of the table were empty, and questions were being fired Sylwia's way from across the table.

Hoo did ye get on the boat?

Did onybody almost catch ye?

Were ye really gan to try bide doon there until we docked somewye?

Far did ye go to the toilet?

Just avoid last ice cubicle, Sylwia said. It had nithing stored in it anyways.

All of the quines bar Sandra were howling with laughter again.

I'm needing oot for a fag, Sandra said quietly. When no one budged, she slammed a fist down on the table. I said, I'm needing oot for a fag!

The table turned quiet as Isobel and Rachel slid out into the galley and Sandra headed past Charlene and Sylwia, out through the door onto deck without a backwards glance.

Jesus, fit's her problem? Denise said, her eyes darting around the room.

She think I steal her job, Sylwia said. You ken us foreigners, we love to steal shit jobs in factories. Our favourite.

Isobel collected up all the dishes and headed through the galley.

Right, I think it's aboot time to get this show on the road, Charlene said. She headed up to wheelhouse alone and switched the engine back on. It was dark outside, and she could see the lights of another fishing trawler in the distance. She thought of the big orange net hundreds of feet below it, scooping up every living thing in sight except for the few smaller species that could slip through the little diamond-shaped openings to freedom.

Her thoughts were interrupted by the realisation that Sandra was sitting directly in front of the wheelhouse on the deck chair, only her puffs of smoke visible from where Charlene stood. If she hadn't taped over the broken window, she would have tried to shout round to Sandra, tried to get her to speak and sort things out. But for now, she'd just have to leave her to simmer away and hope that she didn't boil over again.

The boat began to rock faster now as it cut through the waves. They just had to make it through the next day or so and then they'd be back on land and Sandra would be a foreigner for the first time in her life.

Moby Dickheads

Doug Johnstone

'Call me Ishmael, ya cunt.'

This is Davey, off his nut as usual. He's been reading Moby Dick like it's fucking hardcore porn. We got it in English class, for fuck's sake, but he's the only cunt that finished it. So now he wants everyone to call him Ishmael. He tried calling me Queequeg for a bit, but I told him he could stick Queequeg up his fucking arse.

So we're here on Porty Beach, a bit steaming, down to see the whale. Aye, a real fucking whale, washed up a hundred yards from my house on the prom. It was there when I woke up this morning. Should've seen Davey when I told him about it, totally lost his shit, going on about the great white whale, like it was a sign. A portent, he said. Fucking 'portent'.

Anyway, the whale isnae great or white, it's black and as dead as that Melville cunt who wrote Moby Dick. Just a massive suicidal fish.

'C'mon, Davey, let's shred,' I says.

Davey's standing right next to the thing, slapping its belly. It's lying on its side like it's just sleeping.

'Wakey, wakey,' he says.

Some council guys came down this morning and put tape around the thing until they work out what to do with it. I step over the tape, closer to Davey and the whale. Davey's cuddling the fucking thing now, arms around it. I look back at the prom to see if anyone's watching but it's empty this time of night, all right-minded cunts in their scratchers.

'Come on, Davey, fuck's sake.'

He stares at me with that look he gets. I swear he's lost the plot. Fuck knows why I hang around with this prick anymore.

'Help me up,' he says.

'What?'

'I want to get on it. Give us a foot up.'

'Fuck off.'

'Do it,' he says.

I walk over and help him up. The whale is fucking stinking, by the way, reeking like the back of a fish shop on a sunny day. I'm close to puking.

Davey grabs my hand and hauls me up on top of the thing with him. I thought it would be slimy but it's more like rubber, like a bouncy castle. The way it's lying, we're kinda on the side of its belly. I can see a patch of skin that's a different colour to the rest of it, like a cut or a sore. Maybe that's how the fucker died.

Davey starts jumping up and down like a mad cunt.

'Riding the great white whale,' he shouts.

I look around again but there's no one here, no other cunt daft enough to be pissing about with a dead whale at three in the morning.

His jumps send ripples under my feet. I peer over the other side at the whale's head and spot the blowhole. From here it looks a bit like a fanny. Davey follows my gaze and sees it too. He smiles at me.

'You thinking what I'm thinking?' he says.

I know exactly what he's thinking, and I guarantee I am not thinking the same fucking thing.

'Fuck off, Davey,' I says.

He stares at the blowhole for a long time.

'I'm gonna do it,' he says.

'I'm out of here,' I says, and I mean it. I'm no standing around while he sexually abuses a dead fucking fish.

I'm get ready to jump off as Davey starts walking the other way towards the blowhole, undoing his belt. He takes one step then another. Then on his third step he stands on the discoloured bit of skin and his foot goes right through, it just gives way like he's on thin ice at Figgy Park. His leg disappears into the fucking thing, then the other leg as the whale's body opens right up, a massive gash along the side of its belly. I wobble as the gash spreads under my feet and then I fall into the fucking thing myself.

There's a rush of hot, stinking air and a spray of whale shite and piss and blood and fuck knows what else as I topple into the guts of the fucking thing next to Davey. A ton of it goes in my mouth and my eyes and up my fucking nose as my body sinks into the whale right up to my tits. I feel it squelch in my trainers and seep inside my boxers. I wipe at my eyes and spit. The fucking reek, man, Jesus. My stomach goes tight.

When I get my eyes open I see Davey standing next to me, up to his oxsters in the same shite, his face red and sticky and his eyes manic, like that lassie at the end of Carrie.

I'm ready to punch the cunt when he starts laughing his arse off like it's the biggest joke in the world.

'Fuck's sake, Davey, look at us,' I says.

He stops laughing and stares at me.

'I told you,' he says. 'Call me Ishmael, ya cunt.'

Demolition

Ronnie McCluskey

'My favourite poet is dead,' she tells me, swigging from a can of Strongbow Dark Fruit. She's sitting on the windowsill.

'Really?' I ask, struggling to frame a reply. She's peering down into the empty courtyard, a breeze making the curtains coil around her. It's early morning and for some reason both of us are awake.

She sighs. 'Maybe we're not right for each other.'

When I process this, I can't help but laugh. It sounds too dramatic. 'Yeah, maybe,' I say, and she passes me the can. I take a sip; it tastes like tonic wine.

'Are we going to the demolition?'

'Is there time?'

She sighs again. I don't know why she's upset. I met her a month ago, when I was bombed out of my gourd and drifting in the ether. I can't remember how our paths crossed, but I know I told her lies, throwaway stuff that was said neither to prove a thing or elicit a reaction, just churned out without motive or attention. I remember, the morning after that first night, she asked me to show her my 'crocodile skin iPad cover' and I could do nothing but hem and haw and tell her, 'Ah, it'll turn up,' all the while attempting to choke back laughter as she gazed innocently at me from the divan in the corner.

There's nothing innocent about her now. Her deportment might still be little girl lost – she brings her knees up to her chin, gripping them with her hands, her backside so small she can rest comfortably on the narrow windowsill – but when our eyes lock, hers flickering like the flame of a candle, she sees only a vacuum, a fuck-up she must soon be rid of. Me, I'm too hungover to care. I see a peaches-and-cream complexion, a pair of baby blues, but mostly I see a sad, silent girl striding into the annals of my past.

'We could watch it from here,' I offer after a time. 'Fair enough view.'

'I want to see it up close,' she says quietly, staring up at me. The hulk of the tower block rests on her shoulder, its ruined facade rendered uglier by the solemnity of her expression. I'm looking forward to watching it get pulled down.

'As you wish,' I say, bowing, but she's staring back out of the window again. With a great expenditure of energy, I force myself off the couch and glance over her shoulder. She's watching two pigeons scrap over a piece of stale bread. I place a hand on the nape of her neck, but it feels ridiculous – like something a parent would do. Her bare skin is cold to the touch, a jut of clavicle bone pricking the palm of my hand. She's skinny as a rail; her head looks big on her body, like a matchstick head.

'OK,' I tell her. 'Let's go.'

*

Last night was a good night. I got myself shopped for stealing a woman's handbag and spent the night in the cells. Truth be told I hadn't stolen a thing, least no the way I said I had, hooking my foot around the strap and pulling it toward me from under the old dear's seat on the top deck of the bus. Nah, she'd just left it lying when she got off. I couldn't believe my luck as I watched her rise and amble down the gangway, and I had to stop myself from saying, 'Hey missus, you've forgot yer bag,' had to cool my jets and say, 'Wait a minute, Sammy, there could be a few nicker out of this for ye, son,' kinda like I was coaching myself, ken?

In the bright purple purse, though, there was just a single note – a tenner and no even crisp but crimped and soiled and torn at one edge – but it was still something, so I got off the bus in the town and went into McDonalds and bought myself a hamburger. The wee lassie serving us looked terrified and I wondered what I must look like, five nights straight on the street, togs stained with all manner of filth, and attempting to calm her I said, 'I remember when the first ever McDonalds opened in Scotland,' but she just looked at me, biting her lip, then disappeared ben the back until my food was ready. I'm much too used to it to take offence, and anyway the only thing in my head was hunger.

When I'd scranned down the burger and chips, I sipped my coffee, pushing it around my mouth, and watched the pedestrians go past on Jamaica Street, mostly commuters on their way to work, guys in shirts and ties and with satchels swinging at their hips, the women seemingly more harried than the men. That tenner is nearly bust now, I thought, and the bank cards weren't any use to me. I had trousered the contents of the purse and hidden the bag under a manhole cover – easiest way to get yourself nicked is to be a man waltzing about the place with a fuckin' handbag under your arm – but right then, scrutinising the leftover change in my hand, dobbing myself in didn't seem like a bad idea. I've done it before when I've needed a bed for the night and a plate of food, but it's no so easy - you really have to convince the bastards that it's worthwhile keeping you in. Half the time they just pap you out for wasting their time.

I decided it was too early to boost through to Govan to the cop shop, so I dragged the arse out of drinking that coffee and, when sure no-one was looking, inspected again the contents of the purse, which didn't amount to much – a Mecca membership card, a library card, a bus ticket. Poor old bird probably had dementia or something. If there was an item with her name and address on it I could track her down and play the Good Samaritan, maybe even claim a reward, but it's just my bloody luck. Out the window, a double decker bus pushes off as the traffic lights turn green, and a teenager in a pale blue pullover gives me the Vicky. Seems like a bad fuckin' omen, I think, resolving to travel in the direction of Govan after all, as if moving toward salvation, a spring in the middle of the dusty desert.

*

No getting around it, I was obsessed with her. Girl had her claws into me and didn't even know it. That's if she was aware of my existence at all, which I doubt – unless she recalled the time I entered the office kitchen and she was brewing a coffee, turned to me, said good morning as I opened the fridge. Red-haired girl like that, in an office where nobody seemed to speak to one another, just sat in their particleboard prisons squinting in the glow of their monitors, ducking out periodically to puff a fag by the bin shed, you couldn't blame me. The problem, or should I say one of the problems, the main one, is that I'm married. I wonder if through the prism of our circumstances – my being a married man, her being a good decade younger – I'm exaggerating this infatuation, but whatever way you choose to slice it, I've got it bad and for months I think about her, chasing away fantasies then allowing them to populate a crawl space in my mind where no-one is allowed to tread. Each morning, when I arrive at work, I stow my lunch in the fridge, hoping to encounter her, before logging onto my computer and checking the rota to check if she's on shift. I reread mass emails sent from her account, open the leave allocations to see if she's arranged time off. Pretty soon I've Googled her, memorised her LinkedIn, I'm bouncing from her Twitter to her Instagram via her personal blog. If you think this shit is enjoyable, you're wrong: it rips me up. I love my wife, but I'm smitten like a fucking teenager, and compounding this whole tableaux are the immense feelings of shame that besiege me each time I perform one such 'investigation'. I'm paranoid my wife will learn of these deceptions, but somehow I manage to conceal it from her, displaying a hitherto unknown knack for brinkmanship that only serves to make me bitter about being such a duplicitous sleazebag.

I can't decide whether it would be better or worse if it was a physical thing – if she was just some hussy, the lascivious tart on the office night-out who necks a bottle of wine before everyone's finished the starters. But it's not like that. Combing her Twitter, which she uses as a kind of mood board on which to plaster declarative statements and cryptic slogans, I start to like her. She's clever and funny in a wry, self-deprecating way, generous and good-natured and blessed with sound judgement. Moreover, her taste in everything from films to art is strikingly similar to my own; she's idolatrous of Plath and Cézanne, writes that reading The Great Gatsby as an undergrad changed her life. Even long-held bugbears – the fact that she hashtags the shit out of everything (#perty, #gadz, #aye, #decisions, #wiwt, #higherground) and frequently posts pictures of her own face – fail to bother me, like droplets of rain trickling down the face of a man clutching a winning lottery ticket.

Anyway, this whole farce – because I don't delude myself into thinking it's anything other than a farce, and a most tragicomic one at that – lasts for about a year, by which time she has left the company and dyed her hair blonde and all but abandoned writing her blog, a fact she laments about once a week on Twitter, instructing herself to do better. It's Sunday, the wife is down south with her work, and I'm dicking around on the computer, trying to get some work done, when I click onto her Facebook and see that she's posted a status update seconds before, announcing that she's on her way to Govan to watch a block of high-rise flats get demolished (what she actually says is 'blown up', which makes me laugh out loud, though I'm not sure why). I think, Should I?, but before I can talk myself out of it I'm pulling on a jacket, scanning for the car keys. In about a minute I'm cutting through traffic, guided by a clarion call that I realise, upon slowing for a pelican crossing, is the sound of my own madcap heart beating like a military drum.

*

When we arrive, there's a sizeable crowd gathered behind cordons skirting the edge of a patch of spare ground, and everything just seems too still and quiet, hushed, so that when I slam the car door just about everyone in attendance turns around, dismayed. Without a word, Lisa moves towards them, craning her neck to stare up at the 18-storey Housing Association building, no readable expression on her face but her mouth opening slightly as if perhaps stunned or struggling for breath. I look up too, but I've seen it a million times before; I want to fast-forward to the moment it sinks into its own footprint, be done with it, go home. I'm in a foul mood, there's no denying it, and Lisa giving me the cold shoulder, though I shouldn't care, only exacerbates my distemper.

We join the throng behind the barriers, finding a spot from which to enjoy a view of the tower unhindered by the backs of people's heads. Workmen or stewards, in bright orange jackets and hard hats and steel toe-cap boots, are milling around us, on our side of the exclusion zone, talking quietly into handheld radios. The winter sky hemming the tower block is cold and grey, populated by clouds that resemble gruel poured from a cement mixer, and Lisa takes my hand for a moment at the edge of the spare ground, grips the fingers tightly, lets go.

'Did that drink take the edge off?' I ask, wrapping my arms around her. She wrinkles her nose in distaste, says it didn't, claims she feels like a fucking alkie.

'You're too young to be an alkie,' I reason. 'You've yet to become a reprobate, let alone an alkie.'

She doesn't answer that, which is probably just as well since I don't know what the fuck I'm talking about. It's freezing out here. Vapour escapes my mouth like warm air from a central heating flue, dissipates as it floats upwards. I notice a cameraman nearby, filming an old couple with their backs to the high-rise. A female reporter holds a microphone across the elder woman's chest, under the man's chin. 'We've lived there, och, about forty years, eh, Ruth?'

Ruth looks sceptical. 'I don't think it's as long as that, Tam.'

Tam adjusts his bunnet and continues without breaking stride. 'Anyway, it's been a long time, hen. You'd be hard put to find anybody else up that close as long as we were.'

'And is this, in a manner of speaking, the end of an era for you?' asks the reporter, her eyes glittering falsely.

'Hey, I wouldny say that!' Tam whickers, nudging his wife. 'There's life in us yet!'

'He's lightning in a bottle, this one,' says Ruth after a while, but not like she considers that a good thing. When the reporter terminates the interview, Tam jams a fag in his mouth, labouring to get the striking wheel on his lighter going. I wonder if Lisa's been paying attention to the old codgers, but I refrain from asking her.

*

The woman polis who gave me a bed for the night reminded me of a nurse down in London who helped heal my feet when they got infested with maggots. They didn't look alike or share the same accent, so I suppose it's just the generosity they showed what makes me cast them in the same light. That time with the maggots I was at my lowest ebb, but she barely bat an eyelid as she took my feet in hands slick with lotion, tracing her thumb along the rough balls of the heels. The way she worked a pumice stone on the soles, you'd have thought she'd been doing it for years, as if maybe it was a skill passed along her bloodline. She didn't grudge it either, you could tell that just by looking at her, and when she remarked, 'You'll feel better soon, I promise,' there was a ring of truth to the words I hadn't expected.

'So when you stole it, what did she do?' the woman polis asked, clicking on a silver ballpoint pen, and as I paused, sorting the story I'd come up with, she put the pen down on her jotter and said, 'Do you need something to eat? You look like you could do with a square meal.' It has a redeeming effect on you, a question like that, ken? I don't think I even answered her.

Doesn't last for long though, does it? Best sleep in donkey's years, but click your fingers and it's morning – got to take your dog and pony show elsewhere, cos there's no room at the inn. A big beefy guy collects me from the cell and tells me the lady is coming in for her bag, that she's glad I owned up; but he says it like he knows I'm no the reformed character she thinks.

'I'm really sorry,' I say.

'Sorry for spending what little money she had in her purse?' He holds up a hand as I go to reply. 'Never mind. I'll pass on your...sincere apologies. Have a good day.'

I think about going for a walk in Bellahouston Park but there's a couple of yahoos lingering in front of the gates, glaring at passersby, so I turn on my heels and walk down the road, past a retail park, listening to the rhythm of my footsteps on the tarmac and wishing they'd given me a coffee before slinging me out. Ah, fuck it, I think, noticing a crowd of punters gathered outside a block of ruined flats. Thinking I might be able to tap a fag, or even some spare change, I cross the road in a hurry.

*

It takes longer than I expect to get there; I'm not used to driving in this part of town and traffic lights throw up crimson blockades at every opportunity. When I arrive, I park the motor beside a grass verge, under a tree, and join a small crowd positioned quite far back from what I assume is the building in question. I'm kind of jittery, to tell the truth; I'll get repetitive strain injury if I run my hand through my hair one more fucking time. When some gadge in a rumpled suit approaches me to ask for a cigarette, I'm almost glad of an excuse to occupy my fingers. For some reason I don't just hand him one of the Benson & Hedges I extract from the packet; I flip it around in my fingers and wedge it between his pinched lips, spark it for him too.

'God bless you,' he says, stunned.

'God's got nothing to do with it,' I tell him, dropping the crumpled packet – there's maybe two left – into his breast pocket, leaving him there, awestruck, to find her.

When I do, though – she's stood about thirty yards away, next to a tall, skeletal guy in a Berghaus fleece – the old gadge appears like an apparition by my side, blowing wisps of smoke that drift slowly across my field of vision. Everyone is silent. I get the feeling this demolition is already under way and I'm intruding somehow. I ignore the gadge, who is mumbling something about how he's grateful for the smokes but could I spare any coppers, and keep my gaze trained on Lisa. It seems like she's staring back at me for a minute, realisation dawning on her face, but then I become aware that it's the unkempt man to my right she's looking at, the guy in the rumpled suit. Why? I can't say, but she seems to find him a damn sight more interesting than me. Right then, the building begins to crumble.

*

'That's my da,' she says disbelievingly, the words too close to silence for the boy at her back to snap from his stupor (he's wishing they'd watched from student halls, thinking the drama of the event would be heightened if he were stoned), and just as that line is out, circulating in the fresh air for a second, and before the man she is looking at – it must be him, those eyes, the slight stoop – glances round at her, his head turning by degrees like an old, slow-wheeling fan, a series of cracks shatters the stillness and silence more conclusively than a gun or a backfiring car engine or a thousand screaming banshees ever could. A great whoosh and a sound like heaves of sand rushing downward through a tube amid popping and bursting and crackling and people (how could you even hear them?) all around taking a sharp intake of breath. It was definitely him, she was convinced, but she didn't look back, not now, at this moment, with the whole sky, it seemed, tumbling to earth, but what really was external cladding and steel support columns and stripped-down kitchen units, keeling and crushing, cross-section after cross-section of bricks and mortar tugging the levels down one after the other, all the while the demolition company's wide red banner streaking across the rising dust and gypsum like a fierce dragon in flight. The man in the suit, her father, raised his eyes from the girl (he didn't recognise her), watching in wonderment as the blowdown occurred, a huge plume of grey dust soon rising from the epicentre and coating the witnesses in a fine white powder. What he thinks when he watches all of this unfold is that he is fortunate to be here, to have stumbled across the scene at precisely this moment with no foreknowledge of what was to happen, and that the orderly way in which the building pancakes, reducing itself quickly to rubble, could reveal to you something about the mechanics of the world if you only you let it.

HellSans

Ever Dundas

I'm the invisible woman. So present, so obvious, so here, that they can't see me at all. I dress up the sickness that I am, becoming so ridiculous that my illness doesn't exist. Shivering and shaking in palm tree pattern spandex leggings and a bright yellow blouse with frills; becoming-freak to avoid becoming Freak, I get more and more outlandish. I'm a parody of a parody of a parody.

I walk past a group of girls beating up on a beggar Freak. They stop to stare at me, their eyes narrowing, but I'm hidden: foundation caked on to hide the cracks and the open sores, Hollywood celebrity shades to hide my bloodshot eyes and a pink scarf around my head to hide the bald patches. I make the mistake of smiling at them and my lips crack, but they turn away before the blood dribbles down my chin.

I catch a glimpse of the horror story mess that is the beggar Freak. His face gone, lost in the sores. I don't think he can even see anymore.

'You should be in the ghetto, Freak. You're polluting our bliss.'

My eyes fall on a poster above the girls: **'WE'RE IN THIS TOGETHER'**. Capitalised bold HellSans. I try not vomit.

HellSans is the font of the nation. The majority pleasure synesthetes float on a drugged-up HellSans contentment haze. They all drift on capitalist bliss while I breathe in napalm. It's on the hoardings, xin shop windows, on a discarded newspaper floating in the wind. It's on the roads: 'STOP' I read, and swallow my own blood. The Hollywood shades aren't only a disguise, but a means of protection – a hope that by dimming the font I will dim the effects. I try to keep my eyes averted but HellSans is everywhere.

But here. Here, there's a hoarding advertising synthetic skin replacement – BE THE BEST YOU – and I can look directly at it. I stare in wonder at the beautiful addition of serifs; those simple lines easing the urge to vomit, those simple lines making me feel human again. The text is bordered by the graffiti-stencilled logo of the Elegy Seraphs - crude smudged angels dripping paint, sent from heaven to set us free from illness, free from the sins the majority pleasure synesthetes say we're riddled with. 'Terrorists' is the word we use to describe this guerrilla faction of the ghetto Freaks; fallen angels who take away pleasure from the majority with their perverted serif lines.

'Makes you sick, doesn't it?'

A woman is looking at me as I bask in the defaced advertisement's beauty.

'Don't stare at it too long or your bliss will be off-kilter all day.'

'I won't,' I say, hunching myself into the collar of my coat, pressing the shades onto my face, wincing as the skin cracks beneath them.

'We should bomb them.'

'Who?'

'The terrorists – and the rest. The whole ghetto. The dregs of humanity.'

I turn away from her, almost half-running just to be away from her hate, but the sores on my feet remind me I can't run and I stagger into a slow, stilted walk. I arrive at the bar and I'm relieved to see James is there, waiting for me.

'What's the emergency, Jane?' he says, signalling to the barman for another drink.

I sit, taking off my shades.

'Jesus, Jane. You look terrible.'

'I'm sick.'

'What is it?'

'You're the doctor, you tell me.'

'I'm not *your* doctor.'

'My doctor won't see me, my boss fired me.'

'Fired?'

'He said 'we need to talk.' He said 'things can't go on like this.' He said 'It's for your own good.' Fifteen years with the company, James. Worked my way up to Vice President of Acquisitions, and there I was shivering and sweating, unable to avert my eyes from the motivational poster behind his head: ('**WORK BRINGS FREEDOM**') in capitalised underlined italicised bold HellSans. My face swelled up and I vomited on his desk.'

I take my drink from the waiter and say, 'It can't be HellSans, James. I can't be one of them. I can't. You worked with the Freaks, in the early days – tell me I'm not one of them.'

'It's rare,' he says. 'These sudden allergies at your age, with your history. But it happens.'

'I'm not a Freak.'

'You're clearly sick.'

'It could be something else, like that man in the news, you know? He thought it was HellSans, but it wasn't, it wasn't.'

James takes a sip of his gin and tonic. Leaning forward, elbows on his knees, he says, 'Are you talking in HellSans?'

'What?'

'Are you thinking it? Are you thinking the font?'

'Are you kidding me?'

'Take a moment. Think about it. Are you thinking?'

'I'm thinking.'

'Are you thinking and talking in HellSans?'

I spit a tooth into my drink and watch it float like a Halloween sugar cube.

'Well, I am now, you sonofa—'

'You're making yourself sick.'

'Are you saying this is *my* fault?'

'No, it's all around you, isn't it? It's insidious. How can you not internalise it?'

'Society is making me sick?'

'Society is killing you, my friend.'

I stare at him, my mouth hanging open, blood dripping from the latest hole.

'I can't be one of them, James. You have to help me.'

'There's nothing I can do, Jane. You know that.'

'Jane!'

I look up at a stick-thin mannequin dressed in black. I draw back in fear, sure that death has come for me.

'Jane, *dahling*! Ohmygod, it really is you.'

'Look, um—' I wave my hand at her, 'whoever the hell you are, I don't even know you, so I'd appreciate—'

'*Lauren*, Jane. It's Lauren.' She turned to James. 'Is she sick?'

She cocks her head at me and peers at my face. Turning away I put my shades back on. A sliver of skin falls from my cheek.

'Oh god, she's—'

I push the piece of skin back onto my face, but it slides around, blood coating my fingers.

'You people,' she says, pointing at me, backing off. 'You people aren't allowed in here.'

It clicks. That voice, that whining voice. Big Lauren from High School. I'd bullied her relentlessly. Everyone had. Until one summer she came back from holiday a size zero, gargantuan tits and a face so plastic I thought it would melt in the sun. She stole my boyfriend. She stole everyone's boyfriend.

I dribble blood into my drink.

'I don't *know* you,' I say, clenching what teeth I have left.

'Watch out for italics,' says James.

'*Italics*?' I say, my lips slipping across each other in the blood, not forming the right shape.

'Any emphasis on internalised HellSans is dangerous. For god's sake, stay away from bold.'

And here I am, thinking in **bold *italicised* <u>underlined neon-lit</u>** HellSans and here I am flat on my face blowing blood bubbles.

I see James reach for his phone, and Lauren behind him, her phone already pressed to her ear, smiling down at me. I hear James ask for an ambulance, and I panic, trying to get up. I know where I'll be going – they'll take me to the ghetto, my property will be seized, my savings will be used for 'ghetto upkeep'.

'I can't be one of them,' I say in bold HellSans. 'I'm not one of them,' I say in italics. The ground moves underneath me, I feel hot, I see flashing white lights and as I black out I hear Lauren say, 'Yes, officer, that's right. She's a terrorist. An Elegy Seraph, for sure.'

Stadt

Dan Spencer

1.

The Germans are wearing black sweatshirts. The Germans are seated outside on the pavements – a cool evening – in their black sweatshirts. The Germans have fashioned their tables and chairs on the pavement. They're speaking in English. No English are here, but isn't it pleasurable being a German and speaking in English with Germans? The Germans understand each other. The Germans take in the cool evening, enjoying the cool evening, wearing black sweatshirts and speaking in English...

2.

The Germans are stringing up lights. They're stringing up flags in pink, green, lemon, purple, black... because something is happening, isn't it? Something's just ended, or something's begun, a moment ago. They're living through history. And paint peels stiffly on the doors of the cafés on all the street corners, and on the doors of all the cafés edging round the small, black parks, where the Germans are sitting outside on the pavements. The Germans don't want to repaint, because something has only just ended, has only just started, a moment ago... The Germans are watching the colourful flags blowing ragged between their apartments...

3.

And the doors of the cafés are open. And inside the chairs and the tables and bottles are intuitively arranged. And the low-lit spaces are intuitive. And the Germans move intuitively through the city. Everyone is friendly. The Germans welcome other Germans in (and we're all of us Germans). They're regulars. They have the manner of regulars. Everyone is like a local. The Germans move naturally and freely and indirectly on the cool and shadowy and night-lit boulevards and squares and meadows of the city, all night, at any time of night, wearing black leather, wearing black denim, wearing their black, brimmed hats of felt...

4.

You're smiled at gently by the Germans. What's the matter? they're thinking. Why so urgent? Why so panicked? You startle them, asking suddenly for directions. They look around, gesturing where and how. But isn't it obvious? When they look back, you're leaning towards them too closely, too worried. You bewilder them. Why your confusion? Why so unsettled? You're observing the Germans too critically. Just let them be. The Germans were at ease, before you came. Now they're wary...

5.

But something is going on, isn't it? you say. Something's a-happening here? A vibe? a buzz? Or was it a moment ago, or nearby? They want to welcome you. Sit, say the Germans, if you want to. Easy when you know how. Nothing so easy as being a German... And could you sit? And if you did sit, on the pavement with the black-dressed Germans, on a makeshift seat, and drinking soberly, and speaking English like a German, would it come to you?

Two Epithalamions

(for Alice and Colin)

Liz Lochhead

1.

Who is it walks you down the aisle, Alice?
Love, love walks you down the aisle.
The love that loved you since you were the wee-est girl. So smile!
Smile, Alice – all a wedding's tears
Are have-no-fear tears,
Are mere tears of joy
To see the best girl marry exactly-the-right boy.

Who waits with you, Colin, as you wait for your bride?
Love. The love that's loved you always, stands by your side
So stand by it, Colin, stand
And wait till, love, your Alice, comes to take your hand.

2.

For Marriage, love and love alone's the argument.
Sweet ceremony, then hand in hand we go
Taking to our changed -- still dangerous -- days our complement.
We think we know ourselves, but all we know
Is: love surprises us. It's like when on the dullest day
The sudden sun breaks through and wide shafts of light
Make a real silver glory of the Silv'ry Tay
And every ordinary law and landscape new and bright.

Delight's infectious -- your quotidian friends
Put on, with glad-rag finery today, your joy.
Renew in themselves the right true ends
They won't let old griefs, old lives destroy.
When at our lover's feet our opened selves we've laid
We find ourselves, and all the world, remade.

Tetris

Rachel Plummer

May we always fit imperfectly.

May we have rotational symmetry.

May our troubles drop soft
as rain into a well, may we
flood each other.

May we empty each other out.

May we surround our empty spaces
with interlocking pieces
that hold each other like hands, may
we mine the deep places
our love contains; clear out
our lives' debris and make
new absences.

May blessings come in fours.

Nasturtiums

Diana Hendry

Love should be like nasturtiums
shot through with sunshine and fire,
easily available, simply exuberant.
Love should be like nasturtiums
ignoring the obvious season of spring,
waiting until the summer is almost
over then going for it, rampant
running wild, catching on.
Love should be like nasturtiums
able to flourish on the poorest soil,
useful and beautiful, happy
anywhere. Enduring, common.

When cutting the heart from a cabbage

Jon Plunkett

Don't just haul it out,
dangling roots
and bleeding soil.
Instead, take a knife,
sharp as truth. Slide it
between leaves and heart.
One slice, quick and clean.
Now, look close. See,
a tiny dormant bud.
Now nurture it. Watch
as the new heart forms.

The Champion

Tom Pow

I wonder what became of her –
the girl in the park who sat on my chest
and pinned my arms with her knees.
I remember the hot cubbish faces
of my friends, as they urged me to throw her off.
I remember thinking, of all the suspects there,
I shouldn't have picked on her: the sun
so bright behind her, I couldn't make out
the expression on her face – as, again, she clarified:
'I never touched your bike, OK!
OK?' Whatever the expression,
it must have yielded quickly to boredom.
She had better things to do.
And she taught me that, clearly, I did too.
From time to time, as we grew, I'd spot her
at the bus stop, where, like salt, she drew
my posture from me. I sought out
the morning's shadows, like a creature
who lives beneath a stone. But she
had better things to do than concern herself
with me. She dealt with life and moved along.
Yet I wonder now what became of her –
bold, lithe and wiry as she once was.
In her sixties too she must be –
a grandmother, some determined career
behind her; pilates and rambling
keeping her fit and trim. No matter,
I can't help pondering where her weakness lay
and, if she ever thinks of me,
whether she fancies a re-match.

Clear Out

Tom Pow

Call it a love of two halves; the first
well in hand. But in the second,
having played so carelessly,

I found myself chasing the game.
I bought two copies of *The Art
of Loving* by Erich Fromm

to allow us separately
and together to contemplate
such chapter headings as 'Love,

The Answer to the Problem
of Human Existence'. The chief
purpose of man is to learn

the art of love and to practise it
as widely as he can. Thus,
I thought to bolster

the scraps of what we
once had: a first love with all
its sweetness and confusion.

The 'we' we were never lasted
the holiday we'd planned and she
soon learned to practise

the art with another. Still,
I wonder whatever became
of her copy. Today

I'm finally adding mine
to the second hand stack.
A few books below it

sits Milan Kundera's
ironic novel on the repetitive
nature of human existence:

Life is Elsewhere

The Gutter Interview:

Rachel McCrum

The Gutter Interview: Rachel McCrum

Rachel McCrum is a poet, performer and promoter. Originally from Donaghadee, she has lived and worked in Edinburgh for the last seven years. *Gutter* speaks to her just before she sets off for Québéc. Well known as the host of Rally & Broad, McCrum was the winner of the 2012 Callum Mcdonald Award, and has performed and led workshops in poetry and performance in Greece, South Africa, Haiti and around the UK. Her second pamphlet *Do Not Alight Here Again* was published in March 2015 by Stewed Rhubarb Press, and in August 2015 she wrote and performed her first solo show at the Edinburgh Fringe. She was the inaugural BBC Scotland Poet in Residence. Her first collection, *The First Blast to Awaken Women Degenerate,* is forthcoming from Freight Books.

Gutter: Gutter: What was your first experience of poetry?

RM: 'The boy stood on the burning
deck

his lips were all a-quiver
he gave a cough
his leg fell off
and floated down the river.'
(Eric Morecambe)

As recited by my dad when I was but a tiny cub. He then used to drop me off his knees. Rhythm, rhyme and adrenaline from an early age.

Gutter: You've said that to you poetry is having fun with language. What made you want to play with words like that, rather than communicate in other ways?

RM: I initially moved to Scotland from Manchester in 2010 to start a PhD. It didn't go particularly well: I loved the reading, the research but I struggled badly to translate that to academic papers. My speech – my brain, really – can be magpie, a bit garbled, inconclusive. A terrible tendency to start exploring side streets and back roads. I found that I could take the things I was reading and turn them back into stories, let the words and phrases find their own internal logic. Follow an impulse. It works best, for me, as the form by which I can take information about the world and try to communicate it back to people. Plus it's joyous. And free.

Gutter: What advice would you give to poets who have yet to move out of the bedroom?

RM: I wouldn't really want to offer advice to anyone but I can say that finding a community of peers helped me a lot. That was around 2010 – 2011 in Edinburgh. The first community that I found wasn't particularly poetry or spoken word focussed: it was the lunatics running the Forest Cafe, believing in the ethos of DIY, of community and taking responsibility for yourself and for others, putting on exhibitions and events while running a vegetarian cafe on volunteer power and determination. They were – they are – wonderful, challenging, creative folk, engaged in the world. I wanted to be part of that, to participate in making things happen. So I started volunteering, and then I got involved with running poetry events and so it started. It gave me permission to do so, something I don't think I could have found on my own. I belonged, and I wanted to work with them, be part of what they were doing. I owe them a lot.

That then led to me finding the poetry and spoken word community, which was invaluable for stimulating, challenging my writing and performance, dissecting and analysing poetry and performance. Also a fair amount of time spent drinking and laughing our arses off. Also important.

That's not the same as being part of a 'scene' – the idea of a 'scene' is a dreadful, constricting, tedious thing and in reality, plays too close to fashion, to competition, to top dogs. Scene and herd. But community is different. There are tonnes of different poetry and writing communities in Scotland – you find the one that fits. It might be a completely different one from the one that fits your best mate. That's okay. Community is the people who support, love and challenge you. You learn from them, you contribute to it working. It could be an online community; it could be a group of parents who meet up when the kids are at school; it could be a group of older creatives. They're the ones who have your back. And you have theirs.

That definitely resembles 'advice', doesn't it…?

Gutter: Do you think the rapid rise of social media over recent years will affect poetry? What should a poet be in a post-truth age?

RM: Bouf! I'm tempted to split this answer into two.

In terms of social media affecting poetry, that feels more a matter of distribution and promotion than creation. Things get shared, people can promote events creatively and cheaply, more folk go to things. At its best, it can enable connection and collaboration. There is the potential to use the formats creatively and with great joy – George Szirtes on Twitter is probably my favourite.

The flipside is that social media – Facebook, Instagram, Twitter, YouTube – can lend itself to a particular style of discourse, specific uses and manipulations of language that more resemble polemic than poetry. I'm less a fan of this.

With regards to 'post-truth'… let's take the OED definition of 'post-truth', which was their word of the year for 2016:

'an adjective defined as 'relating to or denoting circumstances in which objective facts are less influential in shaping public opinion than appeals to emotion and personal belief'.

Isn't that basically poetry? Poetry isn't polemic. It is rarely factual or objective, and I object to poetry that presents itself as such. It's a form of discourse, one among many, no more privileged or special or 'truthful' than any other. The poet's truth, one person's pinprick amongst many. If we start pretending that poetry is presenting the definitive truth, then we're in trouble. It's a soapbox, not a pedestal.

Two quotes from some lads who knew, I reckon:

WH Auden 'One must show those who come to poetry for a message, for calendar thoughts, that they have come to the wrong door, that poetry may illuminate but it will not dictate.'

WB Yeats 'We make out of the quarrel with other, rhetoric, but of the quarrel with ourselves, poetry. Unlike the rhetoricians, who get a confident voice from remembering the crowd they have won, or may win, we sing amid our uncertainty.'

Gutter: Do you feel that the poetry you write is Scottish? Irish? Do you feel part of a tradition? Will it become Québécois? Does it matter to you? In the tension between those different nationalities, identities and voices do you feel yourself and your poetry to be outsider?

RM: Bloody hell. That's an interesting and difficult question.

Short answer, specifically looking at national poetic traditions rather than political national identity – yes and no to Northern Ireland. Seamus Heaney, Louis MacNeice, Sinead Morrissey, Miriam Gamble, Leontia Flynn all feature big for me, as a matter of language and phrase, and as a matter of deep rooted emotional memory. Living away for as long as I have means that I would question if my cultural values (whatever that means) are particularly Northern Irish anymore. Some are: family teaches you how to behave at an early age, and those patterns are deeply etched.

My earlier work definitely situated itself more in Northern Ireland, asked questions that I had been unable or afraid to articulate while I was there. Now, the poems seem to be dislocating themselves from real, named places. I'm starting to feel excited about that. We'll see where it goes.

Long answer, looking more to idenity as an artist.

I've just spent a month back in Northern Ireland, before flying onto Montréal, and it has, once again, made me realise that wherever else I go, I'm always going to be Northern Irish. It's 19 years since the Good Friday Agreement, did you know that? I care about that. I care about the fact that the Stormont politicians are by and large, still fixated on orange and green politics, and that it has created a huge disillusionment, even cyncism, amongst my generation and younger towards engaging with politics. In any way. What I have to thank Scotland for, is an exposure to, an immersion in, a country that is unafraid to engage, educate itself, articulate opinions around politics. That believes that the politicians have a job to do, as does the population.

How does this relate to the poetry though? This realisation – admiration, really – for how Scotland engages with politics came about because of the Indy Ref. While simultaneously feeling empowered and excited about politics, I also started to feel that I was more of an outsider than I thought I was. In a way, coming from Northern Ireland was a false familiarity – same language, same landscape, shared dialects (partly), same weather. But that's not being Scottish (we'll not even touch 'Britishness' as a concept... the nonsense that it is). I felt less 'Scottish' than ever, and there were certain things that I wouldn't – couldn't – write about. Particularly Scottishness. Does Scotland embrace non-Scottish stories in the same way that it embraces Scottish ones? I'm not sure that it does.

For Québéc, we'll see. I won't be writing in French any time soon, but I would like to explore work in translation, whether francophone or other languages – First Nations, for example. Maybe happy to embrace that outsider status completely.

Gutter: We were terribly sad to hear about the wrapping-up of Rally and Broad, and then of your imminent departure. When you've invested so much creative energy in a place, how does it feel to be leaving?

RM: I am sad. There's no way around that. I have beautiful, wonderful friends here, I've had the time of my life working in Edinburgh with the various permutations of poetry and spoken word, and I have been lucky enough to have been offered incredible opportunities to travel and experience poetry all over the world. The activity, drive, motivation of the literary communities in Scotland is amazing. I am honoured to have been part of that, and yes, I'm going to miss it like hell. There are still things that I'd love to have worked on – building platforms for film poetry, ongoing work between physical theatre and spoken word, advocacy for more public poetry residencies (BBC Scotland, get back on that!) and development opportunities for spoken word poets in education, a dedicated position for spoken word development funded by Creative Scotland... tonnes of stuff. And it can all still happen, and I hope that the wonderful community in Scotland keeps that drive and ambition going ahead.

Montréal is glorious, and I am excited for the opportunities in poetry there, in developing my own practice further, in working bilingually and being part of that incredible city. And I get to be with the person that I adore and want to work with,

and I am also very very excited about that.

But I'm not going to pretend it's not a wrench. I'm going to miss Scotland with a fury. I'm going to miss Jenny Lindsay like fury. I would like to come back. Maybe you should all come to Canada. I'll open a hostel. The kettle's on.

Gutter: What can't you stand in poetry?

RM: Um... self righteousness. Which is, of course, an entirely self righteous thing to say. Dangerous question!

Gutter: You've recently been in France working on your first collection. What for you is different about a collection compared to a pamphlet? Can you tell us a bit about the poems you are putting together and how you are choosing what to include?

RM: So very different, putting a collection together. The pamphlets (*The Glassblower Dances* and *Do Not Alight Here Again*, published with Stewed Rhubarb Press under the editorship of the wonderful James Harding) were brought together with performance very much in mind. There was a loose theme for each but they were really there to support performance.

With the collection, I wanted to explore a particular theme throughout the book. I definitely didn't want to present a scrapbook of every poem that I'd ever written to date. I also didn't really have much interest in it being particularly autobiographical, although I think it's ended up more so than I thought. I went back through old poems – discarded a lot – and tried to find a thread, a through line, preoccupation that might be running through them. Then wrote like fury in

France, with a lot of ideas that I'd gathered over the past two years.

It is, hopefully, an exploration of displacement, and how we variously react to it. The impossibility – the perceived impossibility – of two bodies existing in the same space at the same time, and how we, as humans, as animals, react to that. Usually angrily, or defensively. The idea of elastic space. The US Presidential election occurred while I was in France, so there are a few that feel waylaid by that at the moment: I need to have a look at that again. There are also quite a few about pigs, and wolves. John Knox features. A giant plastic tomato. And it has a title! *The First Blast to Awaken Women Degenerate.*

Frankly, the poems all feel a bit pedestrian at the moment but they're getting there. I think. My editor is the wonderful Robyn Marsack and I have my first face to face meeting with her next week. I am terrified. Ask me again in a month.

Gutter: What are your ambitions for yourself and your work?

RM: To keep participating, I hope.

Do Not Alight Here

Rachel McCrum

The best time - those ten minutes before the gear unlocks,
the view from the air giving the lie to the land.

Hold grit hot eyes wide for the curve of hills.
Drink the ragged shrug of wavelets racing from the shore.

Drag foamlines over uneasy glassine water with a fingernail,
then dig deep to the palm. And yet -

craving the illicit place still. From our childhood windows,
we could see, on clear days, the Mainland

where we were always supposed to end up. A boot to the backside
when we came of age -

Get out.
Leave while you can.

Exile yourselves.
Make your accent vagrant.

Untether your compass.
Entertain Portuguese notions.

Wander far.
Be better than us.

Do not alight here again.

Ne descendez pas ici

Rachel McCrum
(traduit par *Jonathan Lamy*)

Le meilleur moment, ces dix minutes avant le déverrouillage,
la vue aérienne donnant à la terre son étendue.

Gardez les yeux qui piquent chauds et ouverts pour les courbes des collines.
Buvez la montée décousue des petites vagues courant sur la rive.

Faites glisser avec l'ongle les lignes de mousse sur l'eau trouble et cristalline,
puis creusez jusqu'à la profondeur de la paume. Et pourtant

avoir encore si soif de l'espace interdit. Depuis les fenêtres de notre enfance,
nous pouvions voir, par temps clair, l'intérieur des terres

là où nous devions toujours échouer. Un coup de pied dans le derrière
quand nous avions atteint l'âge :

Déguerpissez.
Partez pendant que vous le pouvez.

Exilez-vous.
Faites vagabonder votre accent.

Détachez votre boussole.
Imprégnez-vous d'idées portugaises.

Allez loin.
Soyez meilleurs que nous.

Ne descendez plus ici.

Sauvant la vie

Jonathan Lamy

1.

tu vas dehors
tu vas disparaitre

tu es au monde
avec prudence
on s'enfonce

tu crois
de plus en plus
aux fantômes

2.

la pensée est un abri
en carton mouille

la mémoire
chante faux

le bonheur
fracasse

Saving life

Jonathan Lamy
(translated by *Rachel McCrum*)

1.

you're going out
you're going to disappear

you are in the world
with caution
it sinks

you believe
more and more
in ghosts

2.

thought is a shelter
made of wet cardboard

memory
rings false

happiness
shatters

Forgotten Metropolis
Written between Florence and Yazd

Benjamin Guérin
(translated by *Andrew Rubens*)

I

Picture New York in the stones.
Houses in the tuff,
towerblocks in the rock and cliffs
become skyscrapers.

Here, men turned into termites
they gnawed the mountains to take their place.
Houses shaped as galleries
galleries shaped as houses
and everywhere, the resonant scores of blows
                    on the stone.

This architecture resounds with the memory
of the first chinks on the walls,
ringing strikes, hammering jaws
innumerable, infinite, infinitesimal.
Forged with great force, the immense monoliths
cratered with windows, became colonies
        swarming with lives

Each tower a little higher than the one before
Each butte a chewed sugarloaf on
the brink of collapse.

    Torn from the rock,
This rock which clothes the life
of those who wish to build on nothing

This rock which could also smother them
should their gluttony forget restraint.

Other creations, also hollow, are strewn over the slopes like suspension points. Birds shelter there and suddenly flow out in a quickening gust. The giant constructions of miniscule beings, these termite mounds enjoy severing straight lines. Blindly, they fumble themselves upwards, shy of finding the vertical. These splendid edifices are uneven dovecots. Their skin is not clear and smooth like Greek marbles; it is as bumped and contoured as flesh. Their curves swell from hip to chest to offer dozens of metres of holds plain to touch.

So notched, these towers

cling to open air

scratching the sky of

                    this abandoned metropolis

                         *

A geologic crowd of maidens

gathered to hold up

the wide limestone plateaus

streaming down the rains.

This water steals the iron

from the oxide-rich earth

becomes bloody and runs

between the maidens' bodies.

Each cycle adds wrinkles to these rigid ladies.

Each season refines these natural statues

raised up side by side.

Eventually, their contours dried, their skin bleached.

And so hands set about them draw no response

they flake

   – like skin after summer bathing.

Yet there was once a time when these bodies were soft,

brimming with water and life, still wet with their birth in primordial hammams.

With a little force against the coating, the envelope would crack. Life is within. Have you ever touched a wasp cocoon? It crumbles under the finger, its fragility tempting us to crush it, to burst it like the stretched skin of a bubble.

       Urgently

desire, always renewed, destroys.

What is held in these great damsels earthen bellies?

Must we crack the stretched skin of their navels to know?

Pictures and life develop in a dark room:

                 Seeing is aborting.

The invisible, hidden behind this wall, is a void.

This skin is dead, if I wanted I'd pierce it,

from outside break through,

          open a breach

My fist knocks.

I strike again.

Then swing a blow.

And another, nearly breaking bones.

I hammer in turn.

I throw myself, with a dull sound,

          down on the earth.

Shoulders at rest – slack – my breath comes back.

White dust

covers my arm

and my hands. It

re-covers my blood

which my breath un-

covers: white on red.

Pull yourself up and pick a route!

Reveal the red or the void.

With each clink,

the dust tears away.

I take off the dead skin.
My sweat streams
and the porous rock drinks it in.

*

Dig out the rock to a hollow belly to huddle in:
  carved by the men of this place.
  Tireless scratchers of stone,
  here they wrought out their great works.

Some even dug churches, beside each other, above each other, shaping a mass of sites where the
mineral alone assures the harmony of the ensemble, the alliance of shape, colour and material
which creates the picturesque. Such a sight cannot be forced or forged and is always a step ahead
of the traveller who seeks to capture it. Believing he would shape it anew, the painter, dismayed,
settles for reproducing a view. What a triumph of art!
The artist out of work.
Art undone.

No author, no artist, no mark left and
yet: Form, colour, medium
  Everything already there
I, mechanically, scope this beauty
like a target. Gently,
breath held,
the settings are told
one notch after another.
It's no longer photography,
it's a memento, an archive for vision,
an aide-mémoire.
Each hole in a wall contains an archaeology. I record these marks as a lost testimony to reconstruct.
These prints offer us a path to travel backwards. So I focus, hoping to translate the indecipherable,
hoping to return
  to the source.

              – 'To write is to expose,'
                 says my guide.

This story, then? What is it? Is writing still possible?
I feel I face a board bleached white by chalk rewritings,
by lines
Days ago, I left contemplation to poets and tourists.

I walk and I explore.

As a matter of fact,
I've begun my research.

I compile my findings. With each one, I dream myself the first with the confidence of the child venturing into the unknown as he crushes an immaculate mound of snow under his foot. I set myself to noting each fresco, each cross, each site. Looking closer, little by little, I make out the successive layers of writing. We are in a place which witnessed the first hermits, anchorites and other recluses. The history of these often high or hidden places is the history of people of every era who, for all kinds of reasons, had to hide themselves. We are in borderlands where invasions did not stop coming and going as though to keep trampling those who lived here. And a great number did live here, countless numbers. Since the beginning, generations have succeeded each other in this place.

> – '*To speak, one must first listen*'
> the solemn voice proclaims.

It's true, cocking an ear I would almost
hear the voices of these people: mothers
keeping busy and children jumping steps.
On a high rock, a hermit cries heavenwards.
That old crank is answering cockerels.
Creating together a world which is not.

Stone after stone
and sire after sire,
a whole throng
comes back to life
                there, on that stone.

A crowd together. A city
has been filled and lives for a moment before my eyes. Here
I'm a stranger, someone ignored.

> – '*You are no stranger here*'

II

> Did you know the cave-dwellers
> in their bleak wilderness
> undo with a step boredom
> solitude and emptiness?

Rock-cut wonder is harboured everywhere. A world carved into a pumice stone, showing its crevices to be houses. These windows, with no curtain but darkness, perforate the mountain, turned into a wall by ancient masons. Their hands longed to pierce the rock. Ages ago, at the highest of heights, they carved corbels and modillions.

He is one and they are many
I am the stone in the quarry
they may pass as they will,
I will not move.

Believing itself sheltered, in its impregnable hiding place, a mischievous freedom takes
                    – Shape

All of these aligned cavities steer the same course. These portholes, in the enormous wall, are invitations to slyly board one of these cabins – any of them – and capture it.
There, it seems, intimacy could cradle itself, in the safety of being anonymous, the certainty of being out of reach.

> One swells, strong as a bear,
> at this notion.
> They are happy, who, like bears
> survey from a high den
> the world below, and find it
> of very little concern!

Sure of his might, the predator stays back
– He rests. And I wonder which
Fissure around me holds the beast
Prepared to thrust upon us his law
his

    Ferocity

Vertigo strikes me: 'Have you thought of the silence of these cloistered cells?'
How does one return to the world after passing the threshold? The cat mewls from high in the tree and I remember the wooden ladder I dared not descend, although a few moments before I had climbed all the rungs without thinking, in one go without stopping, as one eats a juicy peach in summer, irresistibly. The ground escaping from my feet, I can only grab at the floor, like an insect, like a perching shadow, fixed alone at the summit of a column.

While the bear next door regards me
Surprised.
Beside that athlete, that sumptuous stylite,
on all fours I squash myself down
on my awkward disgrace

        and tremble.

                  *

The empty space is a syncope. What is there to hold? Around me, soapy limestone figures become eerie, like living sponges, torn from the deeps by a Greek fisherman. These pitted characters stare at me and fix me in place – there – they are terribly yielding and slippery. I panic and twist around. I must find a way out, a passage, a crack I can catch hold of. On the other side, on the mineral wall, scratches catch my eye

– There, those holds to freedom, those steps of the lead climber!

For centuries, men have taken the vertiginous paths which snake through the middle of these sheer crags. Yet the idea is straightforward: a dozen cut steps create enough relief to place one foot, then the other. After going up on the right, one only has to turn around and join the steps leading away on the left.
One only has to...
What a joke!
My angel is already singing low,
In the profundities of my anguish
A melody:

                                      – Put one foot in front of the other
                                 And soon you'll be walking 'cross the floor

The proof of this childish rebuke hits me right in the face.
Is there greater rebuke than such obvious proof
Proven for everyone, across time and everywhere;
                    Except for oneself...

Come on, its a stairway, nothing more! It exists,
men have etched it across this mountain, which means
this path was followed, which means it's for following. But
looking upon it, I founder
                    On the spot

                              ✳

Find refuge against this wall,
Cling to it, cling as though to a breast,
A skiff lashed to the jetty
Or a tongue-tied leech,
I panic and call out
I call again and collapse
Buried – alone – walled alive.
Convict or casualty, now I am
                    Fallen

To my mind come the past exploits of those explorers of the far depths, sliding and slipping away
in potholing caverns. Where is the light well that will guide me to the surface once more, the
pathway of Ariadne, whose thread I have mislaid?

My head burns. Now I'm a candle
Sun-bursting, my blood is coursing
Stamped as I melt, in rivulets
My life dissolves in barren soil.

A life exists underground and my pillar becomes a well
I go down and
                    I'm afraid

III

Sometimes watercourses lose their way,
and their name with it.
In the mountains there's a river named Bonheur
      – You couldn't make it up –
and indeed it is beautiful.
It leads from a stag's bellow along to the place where it vanishes
      – Le Bonheur vanishes.

Born among this excessive wildness, this monument made of meat, who gives out
      an odour of sperm
      strong as death,
Le Bonheur comes out from the ground, filled with aplomb.
Some have of course tried to exploit its birth's mystery
digging a mine without direction, without luck.
Le Bonheur has lost its way
Le Bonheur is lost.
It too is buried, there, alive.
All weep its loss.
Men wail and the earth lows,
They call its return, it must be reborn.

*

Far off, the old stag replies
to the call of new Amour
which , it would seem, has come forth
there, down there,
           from out the abyss.

So Le Bonheur is reborn with l'Amour
      – You couldn't make that up either.

The original French version of this poem can be found at:
www.guttermag.co.uk/Forgotten_Metropolis

The Lady of Syros

Vénus Khoury-Ghata
(translated by *Marilyn Hacker*)

I

He drills through the rock, drills through the day
in a vertical line in his sleep

Woodpecker's beak or pickaxe
he located my grave
digs with regular incisive blows
spits on his sore palms
stops to catch his breath, pants

This man keeps a forge in his chest
why this determination to unearth me
when real gods proliferate underground
crippled, one-armed, disfigured all they want
   is to climb back on their pedestals

Pickaxe, shovel, chisel, brush
he changes tools the closer he comes to me
   and the sun turns its back on him
rubble and dust brushed away
with his two hands he gently parts the earth
like the sex of a prepubescent girl

He is terrified of scratching me
of cracking my body turned stony
   with so much silence

Pickaxe, chisel, shovels put down
he speaks to me through silica, sand, pebbles, recalcitrant roots
urges me to emerge before nightfall, before the wolves
   the real owners of this island

What does this man who speaks with his tools want of me?
His hands cry out when his mouth is silent
he is not a grave robber or a looter of tombs
   he is searching for amulets
   and buried statues

Last call for the boat back to the mainland
he won't leave before he has freed me
from my coat of stone
a silence four thousand five hundred years long
  beside a dead queen, buried with her jewels
silence crossed by an earthquake
 a thousand years later
Santorini, Delos, Chios, Syros lifted by the sea
crumbled like a poor man's bread
given to the fire to eat

Dried between two layers of earth I felt all the noise
  but pretended not to hear

II

Shut in with the dead
I adopted their indifference
  to what was outside

The living were no friends of ours
they accused us of throwing stones
  into their sleep
of howling with wolves and echoes
of hindering the rivers' flow although
  we'd never pushed ahead of the smallest stream
they said we were rooted though we moved
  from burial plot to burial plot with our load
  of crumbling bones
that we were what was no longer
identical only to ourselves
reversible in rainy or in humble weather

The freshly painted newcomers
  looked at us with disdain
incapable of informing us
  about what we had become
if we were habitable or inhabited

III

Dead yet desired by the man
  who kept on digging
the archaeologist's laughter ripples down his chest
  at the sight of my foot
his laughter reaches the sun and the only star
  visible at this hour

He lifts me like a goatskin full of fresh water
looks me over from head to feet
62 centimeters long and 5 centimeters wide
marble chiseled in marble
wets me with saliva so he can see
  my original color
dries me with his shirt-tail
is enraptured by the purity of my stone
  and how it resisted burial
fascinated by my narrow loins
by my unscathed limbs
a little clay and know-how will fill
  the two nicks in the groin and the right foot

Once the boat has left for the mainland
and Syros is given back to the jackals
he spreads a jute sack on the ground ready to spend
  the night in my company

Why does he ask me my name when
  my ears are sealed
why does he wait on my answer when
  I have no mouth

The nose that divides my face is the only feature given me by
  the old sculptor who took me in when I was wandering
  in search of my twin brother gone to live on the invisible
  side of the earth the mother said

The original French version of this poem can be found at:
www.guttermag.co.uk/the_Lady_of_Syros

London, from what he could see, was the pits. He'd no idea it was going to be this dirty or this cold. According to the guidebook he'd bought in a Joburg bookshop, May in London was the month of sweet sunshine and birdsong.

The Immigrant
Lynnda Wardle

The Immigrant

Lynnda Wardle

London, from what he could see, was the pits. He'd no idea it was going to be this dirty or this cold. According to the guidebook he'd bought in a Joburg bookshop, May in London was the month of sweet sunshine and birdsong. And the jacket he'd bought at duty free was a definite mistake, a sort of light khaki number that the Camel Man may well have worn but that couldn't keep the rain from soaking through to his skin.

He hunched his shoulders and pulled his jacket tighter. Maze Hill; he'd been told; the station after Greenwich. Kieran's house was one of hundreds that all looked to look the same, curving up the slope of Annandale Road. A bit of drizzle wasn't going to get him down. Everybody felt that way the day they arrived he was sure, tired and hungover, feeling a bit strange about everything.

The square of garden at the front was thick with weeds, old milk cartons and scraps of newspaper flattened against the railings. The gate swung from one hinge. Maybe he could help with some odd jobs around the place, earn his keep, make himself useful.

He rang the bell and then knocked when there was no answer. Then there was the sound of a key, the rattle of a bolt and chain and the front door swung open. This skinny guy stood there, rubbing his hand over his jaw. He was wearing boxer shorts and a T-shirt with a faded picture of Steve Biko. Somehow, this guy seemed older and smaller than the ex-boyfriend that Suki had described on the phone. He owes me a favour, she'd said. Just look him up, he'll take you in.

Andrew? Come in bru. Is that all your stuff?

The skinny guy coughed and flattened himself against the wall so that he could squeeze past into the dark hallway. He heard the sound of the bolts being shot.

Then Kieran said, dump your stuff on the floor. Sadie and I will clear you a space to doss later. Fuck man, what's the time?

He squinted to see his watch face in the murk of the front room. Thick velvet curtains were pulled closed and he could smell the mix of dope and tobacco.

Three o'clock, he said, heaving his rucksack onto the floor. He opened the top flap and pulled out a bottle of Johnny Walker Black Label. He'd spent too much money on it in duty free with the voice of his old lady in his head: Never arrive empty handed, my boy, don't take things for granted. Things would pan out. He'd get a graft, earn some money, get himself a nice possie, one bedroom, or even a bedsit would do fine. He'd be the Man in London, working a steady graft, his mates pulling in. There'd be some decent chicks even, and maybe someone he could settle down with. He had a feeling that he was ready for a little permanence.

Here, he handed Kieran the bottle, to say thanks for putting me up. It won't be for long. Just till I get myself sorted out, get a job. You know.

Kieran took the whisky peering at it in the half light, whistling softy as he read the label.

Johnny Walker bru. Ve-ry nice. I like a man who knows his dop.

He was walking up the small passage talking over his shoulder. Ja, we pulled a bit of an allnighter. Sadie's still in bed. Chicks for you.

Kieran rummaged in the sink piled with dishes. The remains of a curry takeaway lay scattered across the surfaces, empty wine bottles stacked around the half open dustbin. He found two coffee mugs, rinsed them and pulled up two stools. Unscrewing the whisky, he splashed some in each mug, and swallowed, squinting at the first hit.

So. Another exile, hey? Kieran smiled, his teeth dog sharp and yellow. He got a hit of Kieran's breath as he lit a fag and blew smoke across the table.

Suki warned me you'd be knocking at my door. Safe haven for all who pass through here! Come to suck on the titties of Mother England, the old bitch! He laughed and spat into the sink – a perfect aim. So. What's the sorry tale bru?

The thing was, he was here now. There was no point in thinking about the months dodging the military cops, sofa surfing and running out of money. He didn't want to think about his father. Your brother can go to the Army, so what the hell's the matter with you? It was a lot of kak. Getting killed on the Border in some contact with terrs was not his idea of a plan for the future.

He smiled at Kieran. No big story. Cheers, he said and swallowed his whisky.

Rules, Sadie said that first week. She half closed her eyes and recited them in her sharp London voice: replace the loo roll, wash your dishes. Flush the toilet. Pay for your own phone calls.

Make sure you lock the fucken door, rule number one, grunted Kieran from his seat at the head of the kitchen table.

Also. Do your own washing. Here she paused. He couldn't see her eyes behind her fringe.

And rent, Kieran squinted at him through the smoke of a double-blader. How's about £25 a week until you get some work?

Okay, he said. It was a tenner too much, he knew, but he wasn't in a position to argue the point. Kieran didn't offer him the joint.

They cleared a space on their dining room floor big enough for him to roll out his sleeping bag and stash his stuff. Piles of old paperbacks lined the walls. In the pale light of early morning he smoked and listened to her moaning in the upstairs bedroom, the thump of the headboard against the wall. He kept his mind blank, lighting a new cigarette from the end of the last stompie. Twisting his neck to read, he squinted at the titles: *The Wretched of the Earth, My Traitor's Heart. No Longer at Ease.* When a book grabbed his attention, he'd wiggle it free from the pile, clean the mould off the spine and tuck it into his jacket to read later that day in the pub.

Once out of the house, on the way down to the Frog and Radiator, the possibility of London filled him with happiness. He could feel that something good was just around the corner; the potential of money, of a real graft. Round the back of Annandale Road by the railway line he'd seen the straight tail of a fox slide into the bushes. Birds sang; the sounds of spring made him feel nervy and light headed like he'd had a smoke. The problem of course, was dough. He stopped doing the pound-rand conversion in his head. He walked everywhere. On the way home he bought white cider for drinking in the evenings.

Like a fucken alkie, laughed Kieran sipping from a glass of red. Soon you'll be sucking it through bread my bru and we'll have to throw you onto the streets to fend for yourself.

*

That your milk?

She was sitting opposite him in the old white towelling dressing gown she wore in the house, the front slightly open. Andy spied her breasts like those white fruits he'd seen in the Chinese shop in the main road. He pushed the carton of milk across the table to her.

No, sorry, I'll buy some today.

She took it and splashed some into her coffee, licking the rim of the plastic carton when she was done. So how's the job hunting going Ands?

Okay, he tried to not to stare at her tits. I thought I might head out to Abbey Woods today though – you guys want to come? Kieran looked up from his paper, his eyes flickering from Sadie's half open gown back to him.

Nah, I'm too highly strung for the country. Too many bugs and all that rape seed shit in the air. I think I might be allergic to nature.

Sadie raised her eyebrows.

I'll come, she said.

Fuck, he'd hoped they'd just say no. Sure, he said pulling out the map.

He'd hoped that after the walk that Sadie might become his ally. Maybe. He felt a little rush of lust when she held his arm and touched the top of his hand with her red nails. She had on a thin top decorated with tiny bells. He liked the way she swung her arms in an exaggerated way as though this were a big trek they were on. He walked behind her through the trees, her shoulders neat wings under her shirt.

Kieran's okay, she said as they sat against a beech tree. But you can see what he's like. He can be very dour. All this paranoia. *The Struggle is mah lahf.* She mocked Kieran's South African drawl and laughed. Not like you, though; you're dead laid back, Ands.

This all felt a little familiar but he let it ride. It was a beautiful day.

*

Kieran's out.

She was standing at the entrance to the dining room, wrapped in a towel, leaning against the door frame.

He didn't know what to say and his mouth was dry. He wished she'd go away.

I need a little company, she smiled, winding her wet hair on top of her head. He could smell something sweet, maybe shampoo, coming off her. She straightened and moved towards him where he lay half propped up on his elbow reading.

Heart of Darkness. Never figured you for a reader Ands.

So I read, he shrugged. It's as good a thing to do when there's nothing else to do.

I like an intellectual man. She cleared a small space at the foot of his sleeping bag and sat down, tucking her legs under her.

These here are all Kieran's, she said waving at the shelves. Not that he's read them. All for the image is our Kieran. Own the right books, say the right slogans, toyi-toyi at a rally or two – it's Mister de Witt, the great white activist.

Andy watched her pulse flicker at the V of her collar bone. How was it that you could want a woman you didn't even like? She leaned forward slowly, the towel slipping to give him a clear view of the white breasts and their small dark nipples. Jesus. He knew that she knew what she was doing. When was he going to stop her? She was saying something else about Kieran in that bitter voice of hers, but he couldn't hear her any more above the roar in his own head. He reached over and pulled the towel away.

*

Later that week the phone was locked.

Now look bru, Kieran said, the twenty five quid a week is one thing but the phone calls are something else.

I pay, he said.

Kieran shook his head. You *say* that, but how do I know? How do I where you're calling when there's no-one here?

Look. He pointed to the small piece of notepaper they'd stuck up above the phone the first week he arrived. He'd penned in neat little matchstick lines for each call he'd made; twelve altogether.

I want to believe you, really I do, but the thing is. Kieran sucked air through his teeth, mister regretful landlord. It's human nature, isn't it. And you're skint, so obviously you'll cut corners where you can. I'd do the same in your position. I'm saving you from yourself my bru.

A few weeks later the fridge was padlocked. His started keeping his carton of milk next to his bed on a small shelf with his penknife and wallet. He sharpened the pen knife into a beautiful slicing instrument as he listened to the Network SouthEast rattling the walls of the house, occasionally drowning their yelling in the room above him. Smoking, wanking, reading. His life as the Man in London.

Now when he smelt their food cooking, he ducked out of the house, unable to bear another teatime eating a meal he couldn't pay towards. He sat on a bench in Greenwich Park and watched people coming home from work in dark suits. You could imagine the cosy houses they'd go to, smell the food piled high on their tables. He scratched through bins—the stuff people threw away! One evening he found a takeaway someone had left next to the bench. A quarter of a loaf of white bread with a half-eaten Vindaloo. Still warm. The makings of a decent curry bunny, and for the first time, he felt homesick. Shit things had never been this bad there. At least he'd had mates. He was careful never to take any of his food back to the house—one look at a take away container and the prick would add another tenner to the rent.

See, china, Kieran would start up, ever the big fucking expert. Life here is tough. It's a dog eat dog world. This is the First World, you have to hack it like a real man. You're not in the colonies now being served hand and foot by the oppressed.

Leave him alone, honey, she'd murmur, smiling from under her fringe. He's doing his best, aren't you Ands?

But it was becoming difficult to think. Lying here on their dining room floor with his little carton of warm milk and the mouldy books, he felt nothing. Just a vague feeling that felt like hunger. His outings were confined to forages to the park, always careful to leave the house before they did. Coming home, long after they did, headed up the alley on the side of the house to listen for the sound of their voices, the clattering of pots in the kitchen; her high pitched laugh; Kieran's phlegmy cough. The best nights were the ones when he would hear nothing and the kitchen window was a dark square. That was heaven, the possie to himself. He'd let himself in and climb into his sleeping bag to read, feigning sleep when they stumbled through the hallway. He lay listening to them late into the night, trying not to imagine her pale breasts next to Kieran's skinny chest.

*

Then one afternoon he got a call from an old mate that used to live with him in Joburg. The thought of a night away from the flirty games in the smoky little kitchen felt like freedom. That night felt right and sweet. He'd been living in a bubble for months getting weirder in his head as the days went by. He started to feel like the old Andy, back in his skin: telling stories to people who thought he was funny. It was good to be around people who rolled him a joint and didn't ask for the bucks up front.

He was still high and full of love as he wound his way down the empty street back to the bus stop. He pulled his collar up to keep out the drizzle. He thought he heard footsteps behind him, but he was a bit pissed, and by the time he clocked them it was too late, they were on him, three skinny little fucks, the one in front slamming hard into his left shoulder.

Light bounced off their blades. He buckled and fell, the booze in him slowing him down. Up on his elbows, he tried to focus. Fucken lighties, twelve, maybe thirteen at the most.

What the hell are you doing? he said to the smallest one, you're just kids.

They were laughing at him now, circling, looking for passing traffic. He pulled his wallet from his pocket, waved it at them and then dropped it on the ground. He wished he could stand up, look them in the eye.

The big one with the cap pulled low over his eyes snatched the wallet, riffled through its empty pouches and chucked it back at him. He spat. Andy lay back on the cold pavement listening to the sound of their voices fade as they headed down the street. He looked up at the street lights staining the clouds yellow and remembered that his bus fare was tucked into his front pocket. Later as he waited for the bus he saw them in a tight little cluster at the next corner looking for their next score. One of them saluted him with a slow wave of his hand.

*

Kieran laughed.

All the way from Joburg to get mugged in Dulwich! That's rich bru. You Joburgers think you're so tough and just look what happens when you go out on your own. Definite lack of street smarts hey Sadie. Whadyou think? She ignored him and went to fetch the Savlon.

Kieran wheezed. No doubt lung cancer would get him before long, Andy imagined, a perfect fucken demise. Sadie dabbed at his wrists with cotton wool and he wished she'd put the stuff away. He wasn't hurt; just pissed off that he'd been too drunk to handle himself properly. He should have kept the whole episode to himself.

I've got an interview tomorrow, he lied. Sadie smiled at him, dabbing Savlon on the scratches. He wished he could just shake her off but she had his arm in a firm grip.

That so? Kieran looked sceptical, his eyes darting from Sadie's careful dabbing motions back to Andy. Hope you're going to shave bru.

After he'd gone to bed, his stomach growling and his wrists stinging, he heard the sound of them arguing. Kieran was snarling at her and her high voice was thin like a baby's. He lay in the dark blowing smoke rings towards the books.

The next morning he ambled along the main road, too broke for bus fare, feeling the sun heating his shoulders. How was he going to kill time today. Then the thought of a bacon roll came on him so suddenly that his mouth filled with saliva. He fished in his pockets and found 50p. He stopped and took off his rucksack, scratched right down to the bottom of the zip up pocket where he found it. A pound, the little beauty, covered in bits of fluff and sand. Suddenly he had this soaring in his belly, his whole body tingling with the possibility of a hot meal. He stopped at the first café he saw. and sat down at the window. He would write a letter, something simple. Like: We know where you are Mister de Witt. Something to feed the prick's paranoia. If he got enough money for a stamp today, that's what he'd do. It felt right to plan the demise of Mister de Witt on a Spring day full of hope.

He recognised a woman walking by—a girlfriend of a friend years ago when he had been living in a squat in Durban. Tall, willowy, funny chick. What was her name? Louise? Lydia?

Lydia! he shouted, running out of the shop. He abandoned his tea and the roll, and ran into the sunshine. The sun flashed against the glass shop fronts and bounced off car windows. He ran after the woman, her dress a blue shimmer. He ran sucking air deep into his chest. His legs had never felt stronger. He followed the scrap of blue, weaving in and out, never bumping against anything, dodging the flower stands and boxes of vegetables, the antique chairs and fireplaces stacked in the sunshine.

Lydia! he shouted. Lydia!

A Pocket of Air

Beth Cochrane

I buried my heart at the bottom of a loch and I swear every day I don't regret it.

I didn't rip it out, though. Nah, I didn't think that would be wise. I had it removed, surgically, by a professional who I knew and trusted and who knew me and knew it was the best chance I had. Not that another surgeon would've spoken to me anyways, not with my condition.

He was my friend, my good pal William. I'd known a long time – way back to when we were wee; roaming woodlands and mountains looking for wild places to camp out in dens of sticks and twigs and moss like the wild creatures we loved so much. We would build our own houses when we grew up, too, we said. Right by the loch over to the north. We'd have the water in our gardens and have indoor bathrooms, just like the rich folk. We'd have good times and big families and we'd want for nothing.

My friend William. He had grown up to be a surgeon and had all the gear and knowledge and shit that I needed. He could do it - open me up and tear out the heart of me with the precision to leave only the smallest of scars in acknowledgment of shitty years I'd spent since the carefree days of childhood.

I went to him and he didn't agree at first and we argued a lot – 'a sick heart is better than nae heart' – but I told him I needed this done because the life I was living with this heart of mine was no damn life at all. He said yes, then; my best pal William.

He'd always tried to be there for me even when the whole town wouldn't look me in the eye and the men would cross to the other side of the street when I walked by. The same men who'd ignore me and spit at me the whole day long, but when the night draped down and the bitter ale had run down their throats and into their stomachs and hearts they'd full of quiet and curious glances.

This pissed me off. One time a guy had even approached me when I was sitting at the bar, wanting to talk, but wanting to talk with no one seeing or knowing he was interacting with this outcast, this leper. I liked the look of him, liked his cherry pit brown eyes and rough hands, but I didn't let myself get over excited, like I used to. Then when I nodded to the bartender for two pints instead of one and this man and I became noticed in the corner he couldn't have left faster.

Fucker.

I wanted my cock to harden for women but I knew now there was no way that would ever happen. So I figured taking away the organ that pumped my blood with betrayal would solve the problem. More than that I'd like to lie awake at night and not be haunted by the faces and figures and conversations of the men that had afflicted me since that first, beautiful face. Fuck all of them and the disgust on their faces when I reached out a hand to them. Fuck the ones in particular that had encouraged me with their subtle smiles and rock hard cocks and lead me down this long and winding road that I can't return from.

And fuck all of them who think of me as sick and deranged and disgusting. I thought it too, think it too, but fuck them for thinking it first.

So aye, I went to William and William tried to argue me out of it but he knew there's no changing my mind when I've had enough of a thing. He told me to come back in three days and he'd be set up and ready for me then. I knew he could've done it there and then but was giving me some quiet time to think and maybe back out of feeding my heart to the fishes.

Fuck that guy.

I didn't do much for those three days. Sat behind thick walls and bolted doors and hunkered down in my home just out of town. Three days of waiting, not even drinking the whisky in the cupboard, just so I knew I wouldn't miss my appointment. The beer bottles piled up by the sink, though, since beer wouldn't keep me from missing time. It was steady company and there's comfort in the solid glass of a bottle.

So I watched the sun set and rise three too many times before leaving and tracing my steps back to William's. I went on an empty stomach; breakfast and lunch-less there in the cool afternoon sun but ready for whatever pains and itches I may have by the end of the day.

Some instinct made me go round to the back of his house; to not knock on the front door as I usually would do. Nah, instead my feet took me down the side of the house and round to the back door, where I gave the door a gentle wee tap tap. William answered almost immediately, as if the agreement had always been to meet out of sight and sound.

He brought me into a small room where there was a single light bulb and a high bed against the wall. The bed's legs were sturdily placed on four heavy looking wooden boxes, about a meter high, giving the mattress extra height and saving William's back from bending and aching.

He was, by the time I'd taken the room in, standing with his back to me and I could hear him rattling through a tray of objects – instruments – that lay to the side of the bed. Their edges didn't quite reflect the light but nor did they lie camouflaged against the black cloth on the table. Not shiny and new, but neither was I and from where I stood they looked sharp enough to get the job done.

'Shirt aff and lie with yir head closest tae my end. I'm ready when you are.'

William wasn't messing around: wasn't here to make me feel at ease or encouraged, or even be a pal by the looks of it. A cold and unfamiliar professional – it suited him. I felt my cock stiffen slightly and I grew angry with myself.

This'll never happen again.

As soon as I wake up I'll never have to deal with this shit again.

My (pal?) William was still tinkering with his toys so I obliged and unbuttoned my shirt and tried to breathe even and clean. I lay on the bed, within the light of the single bulb, but I didn't look at it directly. Instead I looked to the edge of its shadow on the ceiling and traced its peripheries with steady eyes.

'Ready?' William watched me.

'Ready.' And his needle sank deep and bitter into my arm.

Like yoghurt in my veins I felt the liquid slow my mind and grind down its functions, like a mill pumped by a drying river.

Other faces floated above the bed: faces of men I'd known or wanted to know or had hated. A face I suspected to be real leaned over me, all face and neck and shoulders. It took the edges of light away from my sight. The face was serious – I let me eyes fold shut rather than look and I knew nothing else from that moment.

Time must have passed and when I woke it wasn't like waking from a normal sleep. After a normal sleep I would open my eyes and maybe take a moment or two and then know it's a new day and a day that needs to be faced just like the one before and the one before that. But fuck me; waking up from that sleep was like waking from death and clawing my way through six feet of dirt and worms and decayed roots growing strong in the soil.

I fought to be conscious and fuck you, gunky stuff in my blood, I'm awake and this is my damn body. But once I scratched and scraped away at the first layers of fog I rose to find only grey skies and dead air. I'd opened my eyes but couldn't quite take hold of the dark room with the single light bulb. I took in a deep breath through clenched teeth, a sharp sound whistling through my teeth.

Although I lay still, I felt the bed shift beneath me and I became aware of a figure on the bed with me, sitting by my feet and looking right at me.

William. I'd know him anywhere, doped up or not. He'd saved my neck so many times; pulled me out of fights I knew I stood no chance in and fights where I knew I could kill the other guy. My old friend William was a good man and I was glad he was there as I came round from that unbroken and undreaming sleep.

He saw I was waking and stood up pretty quick, bouncing my feet up from the sudden loss of his weight on the mattress.

'Up, Finn. Git up. It's dark outside. Come oan man, you cannae stay here.'

The words came to me quite clear and the sharpness with which he spoke brought me further up from the sluggish drugs in my veins.

'Finn you ken it's bad enough you leaving here this late. Any later an somewan sees you here then that's it fur me, man. Come on.'

And I understood. I understood why my closest friend couldn't let me stay and rest and recover. I got the danger and the shame I could bring to him and, fuck no, I couldn't do that to William.

He pulled at my dead weight arms and hauled me half off the thin mattress and I did my best to help him but my body didn't want to cooperate. It didn't want to leave this safe place where my heart had been taken and left me in safety at last.

Fuck, my heart. I didn't know if he'd been successful or not but my blood was dull and my chest was waking into a quiet bloom of pain.

'William...?'

I lay there, unsure how to move this slower and duller body in this dimly lit room but William yanked on my arms again, harder, almost violently, and I let myself swing up and onto my feet.

Quickly satisfied that I was still living, he reached down and under his table of instruments and pulled free a jar made murky and unclean by its contents. He thrust it into my chest and didn't look me in the eye and almost toppled me but somehow I stayed planted on my feet. Automatically my arms clasped the jar, saving it from falling and smashing, but I was uncomprehending for the moment as William ushered me back towards the door.

Fucking William, shoving me out on to the street like that when I felt like shit and didn't quite know what the fuck was going on.

He opened the door and the night air was not quite cold but still bit into my fragile body as I stepped out into the back garden. I recognised the place; knew I'd been there only hours before and I only had to retrace my footsteps back the way they'd came, but, fuck, my legs were weak and I didn't know about using them just yet.

'Bye, Finn. Come back in a few days, but rest up, aye?' And that, along with a wee nod of the head, was it, before he closed the door and left me out in that chill air which threatened complete darkness all too soon.

The night had long since grown into the horizon and I needed to get myself together and get moving before the pubs started to empty and people would see me stagger and sway away from William's to mine. So I left the garden and felt my body struggle to adjust to this new state – this brave, new world.

I still had the jar clasped to my chest, almost forgotten in my half drugged and dazed mind. I stopped for a moment out there in the darkened street with all doors closed behind me. I stopped and took a breath and knew William, my dear William, had done me alright.

In the jar sloshed a myriad of opaque reds and pinks and deep in its small depths lay my dubious heart. That cruel and betraying organ which kept my blood thriving and pulsing but had taken away my hopes of 'natural, normal' love.

I'd been staring at this lifeless pulp of flesh and veins for only moments, but the effort of standing was bringing me down and making my feet rest uneasily on the ground. No panic, no worry; only the need to get home and under a familiar and warm blanket. Just like a night of too much wine and whisky and sadness, but perhaps with new hope lingering where a hangover would usually lie.

I filled up my lungs with that new night air and, wavering, waded home on the feet that were fueled by a body with no heart.

Days and nights slugged past my windows but I didn't leave to greet them. I needed to rest and readjust to this slower body.

I'd lie in my bed, on a frayed and thinning mattress where my body had excavated its own dents and dips, or on the threadbare sofa, listening to crackling radio and the silence of my own thoughts. I'd never felt so fucking lethargic. It was like my body lay under a thick pile of dust that had seeped into my veins on that night when William had opened up my chest and rescued my heart.

And by lethargic, I also meant fucking peaceful. I could think about anything: the men I'd known and loved and fucked but there was no feeling left to be shamed by.

Damn, William: it had worked.

As a final penance, a final fuck you to that unnatural and malfunctioning organ that had refused me love and affection, I decided to take the jar out to the loch. I'd take the jar and smash it on a rock. I'd let that mound of deadened blood and greying flesh flop out into the open air. Maybe it'd even get cut up in the shards of glass.

I'd do it on the inhabited side of the loch. I'd do it where mothers and children would look out their windows and see what I was doing. They'd see and they'd know I was fixed. That I'd went back to the factory and got myself repaired and remade. They'd tell their husbands and their husbands would know I was alright.

I'd swim out to the deepest part of the loch with the thing clutched in my hands and I'd bury it deep in the mud at the bottom at the bottom. I'd dig a hole and jam the heart in and stifle it with dirt and drown it in the water.

Then I'd come up to the surface. The mothers and the children and maybe a few fishermen sitting on the bank would know what I had done. They'd see the scar on my chest and my empty hands and know. They'd know I was alright after all.

Wait to Go

JD Allan

As a child there were several Americanisms I didn't understand. 'Way to go' was one of them. 'Way to go where?' I thought. I imagined America to be populated by happy but hopelessly lost people asking for directions. Even to a young head full of Smurfs and Space Shuttles this didn't make sense. Why would lost people be happy? I'd gotten lost once in the fields behind my house and was so terrified I prayed to Spider-Man. So, by a masterstroke of logic I decided it must be 'wait to go'.

Eventually I found out it is indeed 'way to go' and that it's a contraction of 'That's the way to go'. The American equivalent of 'gaun yersel'. Regrettably, I learned this too late to stop me making a complete spanner of myself.

When I was six I briefly took up piano lessons. My teacher was a young stern Afrikaner woman with unending copper hair. She looked like Sissy Spacek. One day, at the end of a lesson and after I'd nailed Frère Jacques, Miss Spacek looked at me blankly and said, 'Wait to go.'

Now, if you're unfamiliar with the Afrikaans accent let me assure you, it can make the sweetest Shakespeare sound like Klingon. To me this wasn't praise. It was an order. I didn't move.

Miss Spacek narrowed her eyes at me and said, 'OK little one, you're finished for today. Off you go. Chop chop.' Slowly, I started to edge my way off the piano stool. As I did so she turned to me and touched my arm. 'I mean it. Wait to go.' This time she spoke with a thin smile. It was at this point my six year old brain concluded with diamond clarity that Miss Spacek was purest evil. She was pawing me around like I'd saw a cat do with a stunned vole. I froze.

'Are you OK, seuntjie? You look pale.' Her voice was softer but her feigned concern didn't fool me. I didn't flinch. I stared straight ahead, scanning the faded gold lettering on the inside of the fallboard: RITMÜLLER. Such a strange word. I'd no clue what it meant and even less of an idea how to say it.

Miss Spacek waved her hand in front of my face. 'Are you listening to me, little one?' Suddenly, I was aware of a single hot tear spilling down my cheek. She took hold of my legs and spun me around on the stool to face her. 'Whatever is the matter, seuntjie?' I gulped, closed my eyes and blurted out, 'Please juffrou, let me go!'

For a few moments Miss Spacek was as still as I had been. Finally, she reached across and cupped my wet face in her hands. 'My my you're acting very oddly today, little one. Didn't I say you could go?' I seized my chance and shot towards the door leaving sheet music flapping in my wake. I was halfway down the hall before I heard her call after me, 'See you Tuesday, seuntjie. Very good with your left hand today... WAIT TO GO.' I didn't even look back. I was gone.

Mouthfeel

Ryan Vance

Oliver Elliott found the restaurant on the corner of Kent Road and Berkeley Street. Another hasty pop-up in the race to gentrify Finnieston, it bore no signage, no menu board. The only guarantee of a hot dinner was Lizzie herself, standing by a blank door in her favourite red polka dot dress. She waved at him across the street, and pointed to her watch. As Oliver waited for a gap in the traffic, a sharp sensation of chives appeared unbidden in his mouth— serving as an early warning of the Stilton, which arrived more blue than cheese. He slipped a bottle of mouthwash from his coat pocket, swilled a quick mouthful and spat into the gutter.

'I saw that' Lizzie said as he approached. He kissed her on the cheek as a greeting, and she laughed. 'Minty fresh, as always.' She looked him over, touching her pearl earring to make sure he hadn't dislodged it. 'Oh Ollie, Trainers? What did I tell you about looking smart?'

'And here was me thinking I looked smart in my shirt,' he said, tucking said shirt into his jeans. 'Surprised you asked, to be honest. Not my sort of thing.'

'Man cannot live on Soylent alone.'

'I think that's the point.'

'Your curious condition notwithstanding,' she said, patting his back sympathetically, 'I wasn't about to show up to a tasting night solo, was I?'

This was Oliver's condition: his mouth had forever been haunted by the ghosts of meals he hadn't eaten. Foods he didn't even like – liquorice, coffee, anything with strawberry flavouring – made frequent appearances, despite attempts to avoid them in person. Some flavours went through phases. A week of high-grade sushi. A month of hospital food, aggressively biege. His early twenties had been characterised by the bubbled saltiness of caviar manifesting each Hogmannay, though it wasn't until his thirtieth birthday Oliver had connected the taste to its real-world counterpart, at a restaurant not unlike this one.

Stairs led to a basement, the décor sitting somewhere between a New York speakeasy and a half-finished public restroom. Typical for the area. A young man showed them to their table. Once seated, he was hit by another imaginary wave of Stilton, this time accompanied by a light mouthfeel of something melting on his tongue. Oliver grimaced, Lizzie noticed.

'Put the mouthwash away.' Her voice like crystallized honey. 'We're in public.'

Other times, the phantom flavours interrupted meals he was already eating, muddying the entire experience. Christmas in particular was deeply unpleasant, like sucking on a chocolate-covered stock cube. The invention of Soylent – that dust-flavoured, lab-brewed meal-in-a-sachet – had been something of a blessing, as it cut out all interference.

Their waitress provided a small wooden board laid with four canapés: blue stilton and chives on a buttermilk wafer.

There would be no interference tonight.

'He's here,' breathed Oliver.

'Who?'

'My other tongue.'

'Oliver, really.'

He had a theory. His mouth, somehow, was connected to another. Telepathy of the tongue. He'd shared this theory only once with Lizzie, who'd called him organic, free-range bonkers and refused to entertain the idea any further. Yet other sensations could not possibly originate from food. A frequent probing warm wetness, for example, begun at sixteen, occasionally bloomed at night into a sticky, salty suddenness. He knew what that was. Unmistakable. Personally, Oliver preferred to spit, but each to their own.

By the bar, a wine glass and teaspoon commanded attention.

A large man in a three piece suit beamed at his guests from under a shock of coiffed grey hair, paired with a pristine, round-shouldered chef, her height almost matching his, if you included her toque. Together they delivered some guff about pushing boundaries and contributing to the neighbourhood, but Oliver was too dumbfounded by the serendipity of canapés to listen.

The first course was brought out, a bisque of langoustine with white chocolate and garlic, matched with a slim glass of Chardonnay notes of pineapple over buttered toast.

'Sounds like a whitey in waiting,' said Oliver.

'They know what they're doing,' said Lizzie. 'Try it, it's good.'

He did as he was told. He lifted a tentative spoonful of soup to his lips. He swallowed. He gasped. The crustacean wash gave way to a sweet cream on the way way down, at once seaside and farmyard, sending his brain into a strange pinching pleasure. 'Oh, wow. Oh, wow!'

'See?' said Lizzie, allowing herself a coy smile.

The sensation of hot, smooth bisque filled Oliver's mouth again. Not an aftertaste. First contact, twice. He closed his eyes and watched lights dance beneath his eyelids. Then came the wine. Though Oliver's palate wasn't refined enough to pick up on the pineapple he would, if pressed, confirm a light tropical kick as it hit the back of the throat. Only he'd not touched his Chardonnay. The fine glass as yet unsmudged with fingerprints.

As they ate and chatted about their days, he couldn't shake the feeling that someone he'd never been sure existed, but had known intimately all his life, was now here with them, hidden among strangers.

'Recognise anyone?' he asked Lizzie, as the first course was cleared.

'Oh, the usual crowd. Press and foodies.' She looked at him with a sigh. 'Can't we play Guess Who later, Ollie?'

'I don't want to miss them!'

'What about me? I'm right here, Ollie. I haven't seen you in months. Since you started on that liquid goop you don't... you don't eat like normal people.'

'That's why I'm on that 'liquid goop' – you know that.'

'I just wanted tonight to be fun.'

Their second course arrived. The venison haunch was obvious enough, sitting medium-rare at one end of the bamboo board, but the sweet potato purée, caramelised chestnuts, gingerbread crumble and spiced roast plum were abstracted in dots and blobs, closer to modern art than food. Oliver hovered his fork first over one element, then the other, unsure of where to start. Lizzie rolled her eyes.

As they ate, Oliver peered at the other diners. Was anyone shocked when he took a fluffy mouthful of crumble, or a rich cut of venison? But every taste on the board blended seamlessly with its neighbours. The purée gifted the plum a constancy of texture, its sweetness taking centre-stage when paired with the woody chestnuts. The crumble stole the venison's juice, the plums returned the favour. Oliver found if he alternated medleyed mouthfuls with his invisible dining companion, he could create a constant, shifting gradient of tastes and textures. As if he'd bitten out a chunk out of the Northern Lights.

'I have to meet them,' he said, half-standing to look around the dim-lit restaurant. Was there a flicker of interest from the thin, eagle-faced man alone in the corner by the door? Or the two elderly women sitting near the bar? What about the table of young party animals whose shiny helium birthday balloon bobbed against the ceiling? Did any of them seem curious?

'Good grief,' said Lizzie, and downed her wine. 'You should've stood me up, at least then I'd get double portions.'

Oliver slumped back into his seat, defeated. Double portions. Triple portions. Centuple portions. His telepathic tongue could be linked to every mouth in the room and he'd never know Eve from Adam, all of them eating the same apple.

He had no simple method to smoke his tongue twin out.

Unless he went off-menu. He lifted Lizzie's empty wine glass.

'Don't judge, okay? This is a test.'

'This whole night is a fucking test, if you ask me.'

Under the table, Oliver took his bottle of mouthwash and sloshed some into the glass. The chemical scent was alarming, out of place.

'Ollie. I told you, put it away.'

He tipped the whole lot into his mouth—

'Oliver!'

—and held it there. Two round cheekfuls of dental cleaning fluid.

Their waitress approached, concerned. 'Sir, is everything alright?'

Oliver nodded, and and tried to smile without dribbling. Lizzie, less courteous, waved the waitress away like a bad smell, all the while glaring at him, mortified. But he didn't desist. His eyes watered, his sinuses flamed, the peppermint tingle flayed his tastebuds in waves.

Nothing happened.

Maybe Lizzie was right.

Perhaps Oliver *had* imagined every single unexplainable—

'Augh!'

The eagle-faced man in the corner leapt to his feet, knocking his chair to the wooden floor. He pushed his way to the bathroom, a hand over his mouth. Oliver spat the mouthwash back into Lizzie's wine glass and took a strong gulp of white from his own. Under the grape, he felt tapwater bubbling against the back of his throat, a cleansing gargle.

'Give me that.' Lizzie snatched her glass away and marched to the ladies room, returning to the table empty-handed. Oliver began to apologise, but stopped. She was looking at him funny. 'That's Eugene Richmond,' she said. 'You know Margot Richmond? Three Star Michelin Matriarch of Paris? I guess not. Rumour is she's written him out of her will – he's such a shit chef, she doesn't want him near her empire. So of course he became a critic. But he couldn't even get that right. His reviews were unusual, sometimes perfect but sometimes flat out wrong. Nobody took him seriously until...'

Lizzie leaned back in her chair and covered her mouth. She believed him, now.

'What?'

Lizzie laughed to herself. 'Oh my god. When did you start using Soylent?'

'About two years ago? Two and a half?'

'And it tastes of...?'

'Nothing, really.'

'Aye. That's when he stopped being shit. Everyone thought he'd hired a ghost-writer.'

Chatter rose around them as Eugene exited the men's room and began collecting his belongings from the cloakroom.

'Don't just sit there,' hissed Lizzie. 'Go talk to him! Get us an invitation to *his mum's flagship*!'

Oliver had to dodge his way to the stairwell through a swarm of servers, carrying plates of starfruit coconut cheesecake, its layers deconstructed into poetry. He brushed past the doorman. Eugene was almost out on the street, almost gone. The words came to Oliver in a rush, bypassing all filters, and he shouted:

'What do you taste like?'

Eugene paused on the top stair but did not look around.

'Excuse me?'

'That came out wrong.'

Oliver wondered if at this moment Eugene's mouth was also suddenly dry.

'How do you... I mean, what is taste like, for you?'

Eugene's eyes: wide, fried-eggy.

'It's you, isn't it?'

Oliver tasted vomit. Eugene covered his mouth and braced himself against the wall of the stairwell.

'Sorry,' Eugene said, 'I'm feeling a little faint.'

One hallucinogenic dessert later, the kitchen was technically closed, but Eugene bribed the round-shouldered chef to knock up a feast of small plates, promising his first ever five-star review. Lizzie stayed behind also, to make amends to the staff with some very expensive champers. Over this banquet they'd cracked some of their more unusual, unexplained experiences. A soggy scuttling sensation in childhood, the memory of which gave Eugene nightmares to this day, had been from when Oliver had placed a beetle inside his mouth under a childhood dare, panicked, and bit down. Meanwhile, a year of burnt peperoni had, in fact, been the taste of Eugene's chain-smoking ex-boyfriend, kissing.

'Allow me to try something?' said Eugene, and winked. He was quite handsome when he smiled, the severity of his birdlike nose softened by a lopsided pair of dimples. 'Close your eyes.'

Oliver felt a cool lightness on his tongue, a woodsy caramel flavour that melted down the sides, tart and savoury and sweet all at once.

'Parsnip?' Oliver guessed. 'But, like, charred and runny. The frothy beige stuff.'

'The mousse, *exactement*!'

When Oliver opened his eyes, Eugene was studying his face. He lifted his glass of champagne, motioned for Oliver to do the same. They both sipped, then smiled. It was impossible to tell where one experience ended and the other began.

'Not once did I ever enjoy a meal the way I knew I was meant to,' said Eugene, 'Until tonight. It feels less... lonely, no?'

Decades running parallel to each other, but connected, two paths meeting in an impossible space. Now here they were, feeling altogether more-ish, umami for the soul. Oliver laughed. Eugene was right. *Exactement*.

He scooped up the last remaining mouthful of cheesecake, and shared it with him.

On watching the Norwegian Secretary of State open an art exhibit in a small city with an average income that made you cry when you found it out on the internetz because you were hungry, your student loans were due & America had happened to you.

Melody Nixon

The curling vowels & umlauts cant hide / the lush fact / he didn't write this monologue lacks / the ambition / to highlight in his own voice his pleasure at being here the / irreverence he must force for so-called art / the speech making he must practice / his orange shirt & coattails so tight rn / omg all our European legs are tired / we'd love to just / languish on a [chariot carried by ppl] wouldn't we? / w $60 wine or something similar / stolen from the new world he / wanted to not leave home today you bet [/ his obligation only loosened by the sight of the green hills on the other side of the crowd /] the Queen of Bergen stands in matching shoes & kid gloves you / are dizzy, faint, you just want food / we're not real artists

kid we trying to find work all the time now, we / complain always 'bout the lack, economy / too poor to be starving artists, just / that wake at night all night feeling. Still trying.

Inside, everyone crowds around an installation / of ads / Nestle and skiing holidays / they look serious / we say did we miss the point / over og over / we miss the point we don't think it's weird to see ads in a gallery / we've been living in the 21st century etc art indistinguishable from capitalism's masturbatory machinations etc Engels Althusser all the way through to [Cooper Union institutional guy] and Wark etc yeah / go next door to watch the film see Rancière on the artist's windowsill learn / how Norway is so down with us / so down with critical / but / wants to outlaw its misfits / what

is the role of art in such a rich place? / Outside everyone should be dissolutely scuffing their toes / on the footpaths / feeling it / but those shoes too pretty to ruin.

You wish your friends & fake family to all be here. You know your / ex-lovers who can't pay rent, your lover with the small-country-GDP student loan your / unhappy purring roommates /

alone and womb-bare / hyper nightmare / your boys who real worry about getting shot / the dude you were married to who couldn't make art because benefits / and history / want them all to crowd around the ads in this gallery / laugh / feel this indoor warmth / this white glow / capitalism so funny / watch it melt / this the best vantage / take a leaf of the privilege / gold skin from Wilde's poor prince.

Leave the prince bare / the Secretary of State / no leave this prince with the same sheath as the rest of us / tender / like slow declining America / that Trump is real / the erosion of Europe / let us look out at this empire together / postEuropean / joy of the crumble / let us feel the cold and own it / let's stand here naked, shivering / white heat that comes from burn

dry heraldic quarter

Andrew McCallum

'Haw, Miss? 's'at it? Leuks lik a fuckin shipwreck!'
– overheard from a school-party, as it approached the Scottish Parliament

I

the nation would like to pass
to step-we-gaily into the distance
but the children won't let it

they link hands and
heuch! across its path

to break step would be easier than
to push through their rings of ring-o-roses

it is not the children who are ridiculous
but the sayers of goodbyes
the auld lang syners

the tartan of their dresses forces the eye
back to find itself

until the children go in
the lamps cannot be leeried
scotch mist must wait to fall

II

the rampants crouch in repose
on two flagstones

they look pleased with themselves

this can only be because
they are going to dine on the saltire between them
(for what other prey would come
trespassing through so much shite?)

meanwhile
gulls scavenge dunsapie loch
at the edge of which
two black-bibbed geese wait their turn

between withering branches
holyrood looks down
and approves this old heather-hued scotland
where each knows his place

one by one our roots invade its foundations
one by one our tendrils prise the stones apart

III

the doors are stitched in black thread
no one comes to unlatch the panes of stone

foundered on the sky's bed
the parliament settles aslant
into silence

the street makes a playful rush at the walls
as though at a dare
then meekly recedes

even here
something of a tahririan tide reaches faintly
of which only the crags are aware
as they tug this unmasted shipwreck nearer the future

weeds sprout from the tiles
already it is keeling halfway over

IV

it seems to work like this

the building sails on an aristophanean cloud
from which black wherries slide to port

these are the rain-bringers
their business is with an element other than the land
which stacks with harboured boats a dry heraldic quarter

life goes on elsewhere
thrusting the stems of stony beaches out of the waves

in a bank of raxed sand
the seeds of fresh craft have already planted themselves

what more is needed to promise a full crop
rain
the sun's yellow light
a sickle
a reaper

Scottish Lions

Stephen Nelson

We met every evening in Crichton's Field, suspended in green and gold.

Crichton was angry, and told us to move, but the older boys just swore and gave him the finger.

He puffed out his chest, cocked a toy rifle; we were going nowhere fast for that dick.

His sons were army brats, awkward and superior. Nobody liked them.

We were a ravenous tribe, a threat to the civilised rows behind us,

pouring out of the wildness of the rundown farm where we played.

The older ones were tanned and sweating. One of them did karate.

He was thick set and wore gold chains around his neck.

His father was a fighter, an Orangeman who played the flute in the Walk.

Everyone whistled Orange tunes, except me. I sang hymns.

Another lad was quieter, laughed like a badger in the bins at night.

He left me stuck on a wall in the farm one day, while the pack threw onions at the farmer,

and the older boys jerked off to magazines in the barn behind corrugated iron.

I looked at the mags once and felt guilty; confessed to my dad.

He was kind, told me not to worry, told me to ask the Lord for forgiveness.

I did, and raced around to the field that night where our gang had gathered,

my conscience as free as the sparrows, a summertime stirring in my groin.

Our favourite game was Scottish Lion.

We were antelope on the savannah, with a solitary lion in the middle poised to bring us down.

We charged in a herd and the lion waited, eyed the slowest, the weakest, pounced,

tore its neck. Fresh meat. Now there were two lions and it was harder to run free.

One time, Lesley was the lion, but she was frightened, timid, more like a trembling lamb.

Twice, thrice, the whole herd ran past her and she cried, alone, in the middle of the field.

The older boys laughed and imitated Orangemen.

They marched and spat and twirled the baton. They swore like Orangemen.

On the next run, I let Lesley catch me, pull me to the ground with cold, soft hands.

I stood in the bright green field with Lesley. A lioness.

Sometimes I looked for Rebecca, a girl from church. I hoped she would appear and say hello.

I longed for it. I would imagine her smiling at me, kissing me,

but she never once appeared. She lived too far away.

They called me Big Genie, but I could do no magic with Rebecca.

At night cruel boys dragged a brother and sister into the farm and made them simulate sex.
Everyone watched, just curious, disgusted too and wondering at the boys.
They had a gang we fought. We had to be careful. During one battle, I'd hit a boy
on the head with a stone. He chased me through the scheme, screaming and shouting
like a wounded rhinoceros. My dad appeared, saved me,
offered the boy a biscuit and an orange squash. We became good friends after that.

Later that year, my dad preached the gospel in an open air meeting at our front door,
and soon the pack had no time for me. They told me to fuck off.
I wandered away on my own, imagined my sadness being filmed for the world,
filtering on to TV screens so the world could see my sadness,
feel the lonely pain of boyhood I embodied.
I was a one man wildlife documentary, and I knew the meaning of heroism.

Charles the Third

Graham Fulton

On the day the Queen became
Britain's longest EVER EVER serving monarch
in the history of humankind
and all who sail in her
a male presenter
on the BBC's Number 1 Channel
introduced a waving woman who may
have been
the Queen
or may only have been someone who
makes their living pretending to be
the Queen
which made me leap to my feet
and scream at my wife
'Jesus Christ, it's dead poet Charles Bukowski
dressed up as the Queen
or a Queen lookalike!
He must have manufactured his fatal death
and forged a new identity for himself
as the longest serving British monarch!'
I ran
and grabbed
a tome published by Black Sparrow Press
to prove my conclusion
and there he was
in a black and white photo
near the end of the book
behaving exactly like the Queen
with that ugly lovely Grand Canyoned face
and a crinkled twinkle in his wankered eye
that says
'Come and have a few beers with me baby
and then we'll fuck our brains out
and live together in squalor and death

and I'll probably write a book of poems
about it, you won't know
what's hit you'
or reciting the first line of
my favourite poem called
'something for the touts, the nuns,
the grocery clerks and you'... which is
'One has everything and One has nothing'
if it was the Queen who was saying it
which it isn't,
and my wife,
or someone who looks like my wife,
was completely gobsmacked and said
'Fuck's sake, it really is Charles Bukowski!
How could I ever have doubted you!'
and we all lived
happily ever after
except the real Queen who's out there
buried alive in Bukowski's coffin

whose anonymous crimes are these?

Jim Ferguson

who are you
who are you
tell me, please, who the fuck are you

did you die in 62
with shamrocks on your shoes
tell me, dæmon, who the fuck are you —

wise old woman
with thistles in her hair
gave us balloons to soar into the sky

dirty little man
with a spanner on his hip
left blind-innocence with a broken skull

— every trust was trampled the day you were born
jesus nor buddha could redemption bring
there was silence in the forest, filthy shadows on the streets
winter storms in radioactive zoos

be much better if you're dead
no more bushes running red
from your squalid hands and monster rendezvous

— turns out you were a bomb from America
from India, Pakistan, France, Russia, Israel
you were China, North Korea and Great Britain too
tell me, dæmon, who the fuck are you

who are you
who are you,
please don't flash me once again,
please don't show me dæmon   who   the   fuck   are   you?

Herring gulls wrongly anticipate the result of the European referendum

Stuart A Paterson

Today the whingeing Nith,
the sulking northern sky unfold
particularly European blues.
Hints of summer Tyrol,
lush Tuscan plains, erratic
maps of stratosphere suggesting
something almost Adriatic
tease & tempt & peek through
fitful windows of a usual Scottish week.
The gulls complain but really skriegh
'REMAIN! REMAIN! REMAIN!
we're going nowhere anyway
but for the sake of days like this,
the sake of hope, the sake of dreaming,
stay.'

Sentence de l'anonyme anglophone

Lou Sarabadzic

Look   lovely   la vie n'est pas trop courte.
Les juges simplement trop sévères.

Automne européen

Lou Sarabadzic

Si ça n'était pas la fin de l'été on n'aurait pas tant de plaisir à s'en plaindre dans les pubs à Coventry, en France à prendre d'assaut les dernières tables en terrasse, à persister à vouloir se faire un dernier barbecue. Il faut que les mois capitulent. A Berlin comme à Vienne. On rachète des saucisses trop grasses, le boucher fait une blague déplacée qu'on ne comprend pas, et au fond, on sait bien que ça n'a aucune importance. On en congèlera sûrement.

Bien sûr que c'est déjà l'automne. Une saison qu'on a tant chérie, canonisée, que ses couleurs éclaboussent même le turquoise des brochures estivales restées à demi cornées sur la table du salon.

Ceux qui n'ont pas d'enfants ceux-là aussi sentent bien que le rythme a changé, qu'on s'affaire avec plus d'entrain sur l'achèvement du jour : on veut qu'août persiste, mais sans les plages et les grandes vallées, on veut juste entrouvrir les crépuscules en laissant une bougie sur le balcon. À Prague, à Édimbourg.

Et puis un jour déjà il est fin septembre. Les bougies sont ridicules à pavaner octobre, l'eau a noyé leur pétulance, le vent effeuillé la cire. On les rentre sans les ranger dans une boîte, elles voudront rester là jusqu'à l'été prochain, à voir défiler des jours qui inchangés ne seront plus les mêmes.

En passant dans le couloir, on jettera finalement les bougies. La passion restera malgré tout. Ce sera mi-janvier.

Tout est relatif

Lou Sarabadzic

Au Royaume-Uni ma taille française quarante quarante-deux
devient comme ça sous régime monarchique
une taille douze ou quatorze.
Je ne me sens pas plus mince
d'être divisée par trois.
La satisfaction
sachez-le
c'est
au moins
un tiers
d'auto-
conviction.

Eloquence

Lou Sarabadzic

The other day I said the end justified
The mean people
They thought I got it wrong
But they did

Optimism
Does that to people sometimes

Fortune only favours the bald
When he's bold
I'm not stupid, you know
Only non-native.

English as a Foreign Language:
Arguing your Case

Olivia McMahon

On the tape you'll hear some useful language,
followed by a chance for you to practise

It's my considered/sincere/wholehearted opinion;
on the one hand... on the other; in this day and age;
moreover; notwithstanding; nevertheless; by and large

'People are suffering, They've no food, no drinking water'

I appreciate your position; I hear what you're saying;
I agree to some extent; I agree unreservedly;
I'm afraid I must totally disagree;
moreover; notwithstanding nevertheless by and large

'Bombs are falling on playgrounds, on hospitals.'

Correct me if I'm wrong; could you be more precise?
Would you care to elaborate? I'm not sure I understand;
I didn't quite get your last point;
moreover; notwithstanding; nevertheless; by and large

'Children are dying – there are no medicines, no doctors'

It looks as if we're all broadly in agreement;
I think we've had a fruitful discussion;
I propose we defer this matter for the moment;
moreover; notwithstanding; nevertheless; by and large

'We need your help – urgently'

Revision: State your case
'People are suffering'
Would you care to elaborate?

'They have no food, no drinking water'
Could you be more precise?
'Bombs are falling on playgrounds, on hospitals'
I didn't quite get your last point.
'Children are dying – there are no medicines, no doctors'
I propose we defer this matter for the moment.

So Speak

Nalini Paul

You looked into the glass and the glass was
smoke

You looked into the smoke and the smoke
was water

You looked into the water and the water
was light

You looked into the light
and the light became sky

You fell into the sky
                    and the sky could not hold you –

not your voice
not your hair
not your eyes
not your skin – what lies
within such seeming contradictions?

There is no neat fit, and this
confounds.

You carry the burden of three
continents:-
        one for birth
        one for life
        one for death.
It is the last that you like
least, and who could blame you?

The mist of nation and race
fog up the glass, blurring out
the image of your face.

When eyes have gone
when hair has gone
when skin has disappeared
you're left with voice.

So speak:

speak into the gaps
between prison bars
                    speak all the way to Mars.

Burkini

Cassie Smith-Christmas

You shed your skin:
pulp from pip,
by gunpoint, of course,
for you are in a

Western

Democracy

and here,
skin should be incinerated,
immolated;
branded with Robespierre
and a cult of reason.

Faces weigh
hot and white
on your body
yet this is freedom, don't you know,

the same all-mighty glory
that lets us in our

Western

Democracies

watch children wash up
like plastic bags

and do nothing:

for their skin is like your skin,
and that is reason enough for us.

The small print

Nick Brooks

We cannot depend upon the state to protect us.
We can only depend upon its ability to coerce
manipulate, control and exploit us, and we
can definitely depend on its ability to crush us, so
arm yourself sister. Arm yourself, daughter. Arm yourself
mother, cousin, child. Take comfort in your weapons
though you will fail to use them, though you will
die at the muzzles of these same weapons. It is sacrifice we
ask you for, it is sacrifice we expect. Ask yourself
what you are prepared to give up. Ask yourself what
you are prepared to lose.
We only ask. We neither demand nor command
it is for you to decide, sister, mother, son.
The fathers are exempt.

Always And Endless

Paul Brownsey

I phoned Hew and proposed coffee. 'You must be devastated about the break-up.'

'I could manage Saturday morning.' Typical Hew, steering away from feelings into practical arrangements and politeness, sounding as if he were doing *me* a favour. He'd be a hard nut to crack, but self-respect demanded I try.

'So how are you feeling?' I said after we'd fixed time and place, and he said, 'I'll need to go. There's something on the stove.' I just managed to get in, 'I'm glad you're managing to eat.'

I chose Aphroditeas, red-haired Samantha's tea-lounge, because in its vintage ambience – three china ducks flying up the wall, the 'fifties green and cream lino tiles, the Tretchikoff Chinese Girl print – the past is a safe space. And Hew needed to realise that his past with Finlay was a safe space, one he absolutely needed to reoccupy.

Okay, I was also taking a risk that the safety and innocence of vintage things might exacerbate his pain by the contrast. But risks are what I take.

The heavy-footed 1940s sideboard displayed 1950s shell souvenirs from Scottish seaside resorts. He touched the scallop shell ashtray from Largs, a frog from Burntisland constructed of cockle shells. He stared at framed sheet music on the walls: 'Always' with Deanna Durbin on the cover, 'Endless' with Dickie Valentine on the cover. As soon as Samantha, wearing a genuine Norman Hartnell wartime utility dress with Peter Pan collar and padded shoulders, had brought our tea and scones – she makes terrific scones – I plunged in. 'Well, you're functioning.'

He pointed out I was pouring without using the tea-strainer. I'd forgotten that Samantha doesn't use tea-bags, as not being vintage, but I wasn't deflected. 'At least, you've shaved.'

He narrowed his eyes behind the narrow glasses intended to offset his thin face. 'We had sixteen good years. That's a plus in anybody's life.'

I told him they couldn't be good years or a plus, because Finlay left him and thereby zapped those sixteen years into dust and ashes and pain.

His intellectual-combat face appeared. 'There could be something to be said for the view that relationships have a natural expiry date.'

So I opened up on the intellectual front, too. There was something he'd have done in first-year philosophy at uni – something about existentialism, about a woman allowing a guy to hold her hand (with all that that implies) but trying to deceive herself it's happening totally independently of her choice.

I said, 'Classic bad faith. Mauvaise foi. Sartre.'

That interested him. 'How so?'

'This about relationships having a natural expiry date. The lifespan of a relationship depends on what the people in it choose to *do* and you're kidding yourself it's totally outwith your control.'

His dismissive academic laugh politely managed not to be dismissive of me. He said, 'I'm not exactly free to alter things, if Finlay chooses to go off with a 23-year-old intern he's mentoring in admin at the ballet company. They've joined the Western Baths Club together. Both learning to swim.' I hoped bitterness and pain were about to break through, but he said, 'And I doubt if the intern gets paid. What is employment in this country coming to? Bloody capitalism. Exploit the kid for a year or two, then kick him out.'

'The ballet company aren't like that,' I said, for I wanted to do something nice for the 23-year-old intern, in view of what I was going to do to him.

I added, 'Perhaps Finlay, too, will, exploit him for a year or two, then kick him out.' But Hew glared at that (the glare secretly fuelled by his love for Finlay), so I continued, 'But you're still talking, you and Finlay? At least everyday exchanges, like who buys milk?'

'Not now he's moved out to his brother's flat while *he's* in Dubai. A computer contract. I'd never have thought a ginger scone would work, but this is very good.'

I said, 'Fuck the scone.' Samantha wouldn't mind my saying it in a good cause.

His look said he wasn't personally offended but I was objectively impolite.

'Hew, you're being an idiot. There are things you *can* choose to do. Stalk him! 'Phone him night and day. Stand outside the brother's place with banners saying 'I Love You'. Put adverts in the 'papers saying you still love him. And that he still loves you.'

It was as well we were the only people there because I was getting loud, and Samantha called from behind her counter, 'You two needing a referee?'

I said, 'You're quiet today.'

'Saturday mornings are unpredictable. Now Saturday afternoons, we're usually crowded.'

That was useful information. I said, 'Well, this has been nice. We must do it again. But next Saturday morning's not on for me.'

Hew said, 'Me neither.'

'Next Saturday afternoon, then,' I said, calculating correctly – calculating manipulatively – that his politeness would grant me Saturday afternoon after he'd denied me Saturday morning.

Even though there were no everyday exchanges between Finlay and Hew, I took the precaution of waiting until late the following Friday before 'phoning Finlay at his work. As soon as I announced myself he sighed my name with delight as if I was the one person he'd dreamed of hearing from. He's like that with everyone. He trained as an actor at the Conservatoire before going into arts admin.

He added, 'Unfortunately, I can only spare a minute.' Only a minute was good. 'I have to get to the airport to collect Erik.'

Some people drop names to impress, but when Finlay dropped Erik's, it was only because I, being special, would be just as excited about Erik as he was.

'Erik?'

'Erik Willumsen. Royal Danish Ballet. He's coming over to make sure of our Bournonville style for 'La Sylphide'.'

I couldn't have given myself a better cue.

I said, ' 'La Sylphide': guy abandons his true love to chase some shimmery will-o-the-wisp fantasy figure he glimpses out of the corner of his eye. Quite a common theme in nineteenth-century ballet, wasn't it? 'Coppelia'. 'The Two Pigeons'. Even 'Swan Lake'? What I was calling about, it's Hew – but *no!* – over the 'phone at your work is *not* a good idea. Are you free to meet for coffee tomorrow afternoon?'

I calculated correctly that my being dramatic and mysterious would manipulate him to *Yes* even if his love for Hew was as yet too deeply submerged beneath the turbulence created by the backstrokes and crawls of the 23-year-old intern. Then I 'phoned Samantha to ask if I could I pop in with a record I'd like played on her Pye radiogram the next afternoon. The seventies aren't really far enough back in vintage time for her, but it was enough for her that I said, 'It's so love will triumph.'

Aphroditeas was crowded on the Saturday afternoon, as I'd hoped. When Finlay arrived and saw Hew at the table with me, his grin expressed relish for the situation and whatever might be going to happen, and he actually said, melodramatically, 'Oho!' Finlay smiles a lot and his face, with its unconstrained tangle of curls above, still has the air of a mischievous pixie despite his being fortyish. Hew nodded at him, then studied the menu very intently.

Finlay hadn't greeted Hew. I don't mean he snubbed him. It was more as though they'd been together so recently – say, an hour ago, negotiating who got into the bathroom first to shave – that greeting was redundant. Ah, the habits that arise from and disclose and even constitute love!

I plunged in. 'Somebody's got to remind you two that you love each other.' Finlay gasped and laughed at my audacity, Hew looked pained, and I said, 'See, if you ever love someone, you always love them.'

Hew said, 'What possible evidence could there be for that?' and Finlay said, with an intimate's privileged irritability, 'You're doing your intellectual thing, Hew,' and there it was, the invisible gravitational attraction that renders two giant stars helpless in each other's orbits.

Hew ignored him. 'If you were right, how could break-ups happen?'

I said, 'Because human beings are messed up and divided and weak and bugger up their own best plans and get led astray by false images and 23-year-old interns young enough to be their son – you realise he was seven when you two first got together? – who should be regarded as no more than a momentary distraction like music booming out from a passing car.'

That was taking a risk, but I was calculating on Finlay's appreciation of the drama I was developing to override any disposition to take offence. Just for a moment, his eyes had a cold appraising look that belonged to no-one at all but then my new audacity produced a new grin and, like Elizabeth I dropping a handkerchief onto the stage among Shakespeare's actors just to see what they would do, he said, 'Why does it get you so worked up if Hew and I split up?'

If!

'I wondered that, too,' Hew said. At the same moment each turned in his chair to stare directly at me, one from each side. The move might have been choreographed. Actually, it *had* been choreographed, by the common soul they share but which was obscured by all the muck and stuff piled on top of it.

They were asking the wrong question. The right question is not why someone makes it their business to bring two estranged lovers back together, but why people *don't* make reuniting them their business. Urging upon them the reality of their love is or ought to be the default position. But I decided I'd better say something more conventional.

I said, 'You don't realise what a blow it is to other people, you two splitting up. Other people struggle on with their doubts, their suspicions that other people's relationships are so much richer than their own. They see a couple like you two and realise: they've made it so we can make it, too. If you two fall apart, what hope is there for anyone else?'

It crossed my mind, as Samantha laid our teas and scones before us, that sometimes it works the other way. If the perfect couple go under, if seemingly impossible standards are no longer being waved in people's faces, then people think their own relationships are the real thing after all and rest content in them.

Whatever.

I drove on, 'And it's not just other gays who feel like that. Janine across the landing from you, she said that when she and her husband nearly fell apart, she was inspired by you two.'

I didn't say what she'd actually said, at one of the parties given by Hew-and-Finlay (joined by hyphens as symbols of eternal union): 'If a queer couple can avoid falling apart, why can't a normal couple?'

Without any hint he was inviting Finlay to correct him, Hew said, 'But we *have* fallen apart.'

I remembered what he'd said about exploiting interns and capitalism. I said, 'Splitting up is selfish. It ignores the social dimension of relationships, which is exactly what capitalism does, trying to reduce everything to private deals between private individuals, and to hell with the effects on other people.'

Hew said thoughtfully, 'Hmm. Lovers seeing each other as possessing a commodity – or perhaps just seeing each other *as* commodities – to be traded in a market exchange via private contract. Interesting.'

Finlay laughed like a child watching a favourite mechanical toy do its stuff and I said,

'Which is nothing like the irresistible magnetism of true love.'

At that moment the chatter in the tea-lounge and the clink of the china were quietly underscored by Roberta Flack singing 'Jesse', her 1973 recording with its aching lines about waiting for someone who's left you to come home and fill the hole in the bed (which can provoke snorts of laughter, but not when listened to with the heart) and still setting a place at table for the gone-away one.

I said, 'There's a message there. Let it carry you with it.'

Finlay said, 'Oh, wow, the perfect moment!'

Hew said, 'It's just sentimentality.'

'Sentimentality,' I said, 'points you towards an emotion which is truly yours but which you've lost sight of.'

Finlay said, 'Hew will only accept that if one of his French intellectuals said it.'

Hew suddenly smiled – it had the effect, at that moment, of taking his trousers off – and said, but as if to himself or perhaps to a learned audience somewhere, '"Epistemising la Sentimentalité: Mawkishness as Cognitively Preluding the Restoration to Consciousness of Impaired Affective Reality."'

Finlay said, 'I like the bit where the zombie eats the baby.'

Each was half-laughing, catching the other's eye in a flickering silver chain of understandings. An old habit of teasing was now fully resurfaced from the love in their depths. The moment had come to manoeuvre sentimentality into action. I stood up and tapped my cup with my teaspoon.

Samantha said, 'Don't break my china! It's genuine 50s Royal Grafton.'

I said, 'Everyone, can I have your attention, please? See these two guys here? They love each other. Sixteen years together have proved that.' Hew turned towards the door and tried to get to his feet, but I pushed him back down. Finlay was watching a performance.

'But they can't see the love any more. They've been distracted by surface noise and static and interference. By random yearnings for speedos.' Finlay gasped, still more delightedly than before. 'And so they've split up, despite the eternal love uniting them.'

Silence. Some people stared. Some people determinedly didn't stare.

I cried, 'But they just need a push from you, to get them back where they belong. Come on, tell them not to be so silly.' Silence. 'Do I have to get out pom-poms and jump up and down?' Laughter. 'Just say it. *Reunite!* The imperative mood. *Reunite!*'

Someone muttered something about something being rammed down your throat all the time these days, but Samantha, presiding at her counter, called '*Reunite!*' and raised her arms like an orchestra conductor. Three girls waved their cups and said it with party heartiness: '*Reunite!*' Two men on a couch, one looking nervous, one apparently interrupted in some sort of tirade he'd been addressing to the other, looked embarrassed but muttered it. An old man called '*Reunite!*' as if to spite the two women he was with. From all sides the chant came: '*Reunite!*' '*Reunite!*' '*Reunite!*' Someone got out a mobile 'phone and took a photo of our table.

How surprised they'll be that only Hew and Finlay show up in it.

Hew shrugged as if to say: it's up to you. Finlay shrugged as if to say: what else can we do?

The correct answer was: nothing.

Hew said to Finlay, 'You win,' which was puzzling because Finlay had left *him*, but there, those things are all on the surface.

I said, 'Actually, *I* win.'

They rose and hugged, but decorously, as though consoling a person at a funeral. Perhaps they were worried someone might shout, *'Get a room!'*

So I did.

There was a general burst of laughter, and Samantha's wee son ran out from behind her counter, where he had been sitting reading a comic, and smacked Hew on the bottom and cried, *'REE'NITE!'* and that transforming smile visited Hew again. Their hug turned into something less decorous, hands moving like creatures reacquainting themselves with items from the safe past. After they kissed, Finlay said to me over Hew's shoulder, 'Awesome performance.'

They sat down and got so engrossed in talking that when Samantha brought the bill, plus a complimentary raspberry and pecan slice for each which she'd hastily iced with a heart, they didn't appear to notice anything odd in the fact that the bill was for only two teas and two scones, nor did Hew, politely handing used crockery up to Samantha, appear puzzled by the absence from the table of a third plate, cup and saucer.

Shame about the 23-year-old intern. But he'll learn, for I shall teach him, that people's loves are tremendous and eternal; are like whales, Leviathans of the darkness beneath, sometimes obscured by weed or barnacles or sheer black distance, often imperceptible from the surface, entirely unaffected by the surges and waves and storms and turbulences that happen up there, no matter how fetching you look as you stir up the surface waters in your speedos. I'll 'phone him and propose coffee.

Serendipity and the Professional

Marek O Lasce

I reached IJmuden with about an hour to spare. IJmuden is Amsterdam's port for North Sea ferries and I parked half a mile or so from the dock gates. I locked my doors, but left the rear, near-side window open a fraction. My car is fitted with heavily tinted glass making it virtually impossible to see into the interior. It is a powerful Mercedes saloon and has the overall appearance of the kind of sleek limousine favoured by European gangsters and mobsters.

I strolled back along the quay to the Café Waasdorp, a down-to-earth seafood bar where the fare is wide ranging and excellent, the simple fish and chips in a class of its own. Though the mid-April afternoon was sunny and warm, and many of the pavement tables and chairs were unoccupied, I chose to sit inside and out of sight. I washed down my meal with a large Hoëgaärden beer and was on to my second when the bikers started to arrive. Every crossing seems to carry a dozen or more motorcyclists who are seriously engaged in long-distance touring, and before sailing, they tend to congregate outside Laurens' to exchange greetings, swap the odd anecdote, but above all to admire each other's machines. Even if I could find the leatherwear to fit me, I personally cannot see the attraction of riding thousands of miles on two wheels, exposed to the elements and astride a throbbing engine. Perhaps it's my age. But I do appreciate the skill and dedication; the symbiosis of Man and Mechanism. On this occasion, a vintage Harley Davidson with original side-car was arousing much interest. And rightly so; it was in pristine condition.

I returned to my car. As expected the envelope lay on the back seat. Without opening it, I slipped it into my jacket pocket. I then drove with slow deliberation towards the queue of vehicles waiting to embark. Three or four cars bearing Dutch and German registration plates followed in my wake, but I didn't look at them too closely. I passed through passport and ticket control and before long boarded without further ado.

I had a single berth, outside cabin astern. After showering and shaving and promising myself that I would go on a diet, I made myself comfortable with a best-selling detective novel. Hasty resolutions notwithstanding, shortly before eight o'clock I went in search of something to eat. Some of the catering staff gave the impression that they recognised me from a previous crossing, and though I hadn't pre-booked a table, the maître d' of the restaurant greeted me with the enthusiasm and deference due to a regular customer. The wine and the rich à la carte dinner made me feel drowsy so, despite all the on-board entertainment on offer and the lure of the casino, I retired early. I avoid contact with other passengers because it is all too easy to start speculating.

It was drizzling when we docked in North Shields. Well rested and breakfasted on scrambled eggs, fried mushrooms and Cumberland sausages with buttered toast and copious cups of lemon tea, I felt cautiously confident. However, for some unexplained reason there was a delay in disembarkation. Passengers on the car decks began to get restless, and their vociferous disgruntlement well tempered my mood of growing anxiety. I felt the onset of a cold sweat, but eventually the bow doors were opened and the threat of a claustrophobic panic attack gradually subsided.

Once on dry land I still couldn't help but drive somewhat erratically and gave the impression of being rather confused, not knowing which lane I should be in or which queue I should join. I find it difficult to understand why British Port Authority officials have scant regard for the logistical requirements of left-hand drive vehicles. After all, their control booths are glazed all around with sliding panels and offer a means of access and egress on both flanks. I made no attempt to hide my nervousness. Nonetheless, apart from having to heave myself out of my car and walk round it so as to present my documents, I cleared Immigration without incident. Several yards in front of me a Customs Officer took but one glance at my number plate and waved me off to the side. I was directed to a space at the far end of the inspection shed. Mine was the only vehicle there. Behind me a stream of cars with EU registrations was let through without let or hindrance. Amongst them a young German family in an Opel hatchback packed to capacity with brand new camping equipment caught my attention, but then the Customs Official stood at my window.

'What're you doing here?' she asked without preamble.

'I live here,' I replied and handed her my British passport.

She was obviously taken aback, but quickly regained her composure. As she thumbed through the pages of my passport, which are covered in a multitude of stamps and visas from the Balkans and Central Europe, I realised my photograph was over eight years old and yet again felt a pang of guilt about the amount of weight I have put on since it was taken. The officer took no notice. She had an oval face, blonde hair in a neat feather cut and deep brown eyes. A flattish nose and broad lips suggested more than a plain Caucasian ancestry. She wasn't very tall, but stocky without being fat and well-filled her uniform. She seemed to be intent on trying to get her tongue round my surname, which with its consecutive consonants appears so non-user friendly to the Anglo-Saxon eye.

'And the car is yours,' she said. It was a statement.

'Yes.' I said.

'But it's registered in Poland.'

'That's right.'

'Are you importing it?'

'No, I shall be driving back in about six weeks time.'

'I see... So what are you, retired or something?'

'Yes I'm retired, but I'm doing some private research.'

'Oh, what kind of research?'

'I'm gathering material for a possible PhD thesis.'

'Really. On what?'

'The popular Polish novel between 1968 and 1989.'

'Really.'

'Well even the Communists had to enjoy some kind of escapism...'

Her expression remained blank and she looked round the interior of the car, then at me, pointedly. I never consciously dress for the part, but having an academic bent, suede shoes, corduroy trousers and a tweed jacket are invariably the order of the day, though I do draw the line at elbow patches.

'And how long have you lived here?' she demanded.

'What in the U.K.... oh since 1953,' and in my mind added, 'since Stalin died and long before you were born sweetheart...'

'Whereabouts?'

'At the moment I stay in Glasgow.'

'You know you're not allowed to bring pornography, firearms and drugs into the United Kingdom.'

'Yes.'

'Well do you have any?'

'No.'

'What about tobacco?'

'I have half a carton of Silk Cut, I didn't have time to buy anything in Holland, I only just made it on to the ferry.'

Again she looked round the interior of the car as if hoping to see something she had previously missed.

'Would you mind opening the boot?' Her tone seemed to have mellowed.

Again I clambered out of the car and lifted the lid of the boot to reveal three cardboard cartons and an unzipped hold-all of clothes.

'What's in the boxes?' she asked, becoming suspicious anew.

'They're empty.'

She gave me an enquiring look.

'I'm going to be taking some books back with me, so since I already had the cartons...'

She shook each carton in turn, then reached for the hold-all.

'I've two bottles of vodka in there,' I said quickly.

She rummaged in my bag. She peered into the wells beside the wheel arches. She inspected the spare wheel compartment. She got down on her hands and knees and stared under the chassis. When she got up she dusted off her trousers and walked off to a small, wood-partitioned office. Outside one of her colleagues had stopped a car with British registration plates, but after a brief exchange with the driver, let him pass through. She came back with a torch, got down on her hands and knees once more and shone her beam all along the undercarriage. Then she walked purposefully right round the car scrutinising the bodywork. Finally she indicated that I should close the boot and handed me back my passport.

'I shall have to file a report stating that I stopped and searched you,' she explained. 'I just need some particulars, Mr erh...'

I dictated my name and address, which she jotted down in her notebook. That done, she went to operate the mechanism which opened the shed's roller shutters. As I fired the engine, she said, 'Have a safe journey!' and she smiled. Dimples surfaced in her cheeks. I drove away from the terminal buildings at a leisurely pace, heading north for the A1 and Edinburgh.

Some ten miles shy of Morpeth, I pulled into a Little Chef service station. I parked in the lot alongside the single storied, yellow brick building under a sign which read P, Disabled Toilet and Refreshments, surmounted by an array of appropriate symbols. I locked my doors and as before left a rear window open about an inch. It had stopped drizzling, but the moment I entered the cafeteria, my glasses steamed up. The décor was purely functional stainless steel and plastic. At the counter I ordered a tea and it was served to me at the cash register, milk already added. The café was well patronised, but I found a seat that gave me a view of the main road. I lit a cigarette. The walls were adorned in gaudy prints which purported to depict the meals that were available and for a second I was tempted by the idea of a bacon sandwich. It was but a yen for that tasteless, white, 'cotton wool' bread that nobody would ever dare bake on the Continent, let alone sell. I resisted.

Perhaps it was high time that I really retired. Perhaps I should sell my car and take up some proper exercise, nothing silly like jogging or aerobics, but serious walking or maybe even swimming. But then again, sooner or later the telephone would ring and there would be another frontier to cross; another diversion to give the days a taste of adventure. And in this consumer world of health awareness fat people tend to stand out. They are noticed and remarked upon, albeit often in unflattering undertones. They are always the last to be chosen to play team games; yet in a sense they are integral to the current workings and machinations of social systems.

My musings were interrupted by the noisy arrival of a motorcycle that pulled into the forecourt. The rider was dressed in black from head to toe, black leathers and a black helmet with a black visor. No decals and no logos. He paused outside the cafeteria and seemed to study his reflection in the plate-glass window, only to pull away and vanish from view into the parking lot. Moments later he roared off again heading back towards Newcastle, in the direction whence he had come. Of course it could have been a she.

I lit another cigarette. Bought a bottle of sparkling mineral water and returned to my car. As expected the envelope lay on the back seat. It was larger than the one I'd received in Holland, and much, much thicker. I slit it open with my keys. It contained one hundred dollar bills in crisp, new bundles. I put it into the side pocket of the door. Together with its predecessor, I had been paid a very substantial amount of money and though, as I keep telling myself, it doesn't do to speculate, I surmised that the consignment must have been narcotics, probably shipped in amongst all that virgin camping gear by a respectable, young German family taking an Easter break. I couldn't help but feel well pleased with myself. The last twenty four hours earnings would tidily augment my ever growing Pension Fund with enough to spare for a fortnight's frolicking in Rio de Janeiro, or New Orleans, or Las Vegas, should I be so inclined.

Once more I headed northwards and smiling to myself, whispered, 'God bless the English and their repressed racism, their xenophobia and their smug sense of superiority.' Is it traits like these that make them so predictable and so easy to outwit? On the other hand there are those who might think some sort of poetic justice would be served were I to suffer a stroke or a heart attack on my way back home. But then that might involve a serious road accident and unfailry injure, maime, even kill innocent people. Or could it be that in the end it's all just a matter of serendipity, of who's actually playing with whom? And I laughed out loud as I wondered how the Customs Officer would have reacted had I told her the truth about my occupation.

Buttercup Boy

Claire Deans Donnelly

Today we were going to do it to him. Strange then that this morning, I found myself doing the normal things. I crawled out of my pit, threw my school uniform on, heard the rain pelting against the window, and the distant sound of some stray dog yelping. I made an effort to brush my teeth but the tube squeezed empty. I bit off the hard chewy bits at the top – at least my breath wouldn't stink.

There was nobody downstairs – the house lay silent; cold. No table lay spread with freshly baked bread and melting butter; no younger sibling sat chuckling in a high chair; the tranny did not broadcast the early morning news in the dulcet tone of the newsreader; mother did not turn her head, tossing her long styled curls and say softly, 'morning sweetheart'; a cereal selection was not spread across the breakfast table; and father did not sit buried in his newspaper, drinking brewed coffee, and muttering about the state of local politics. I saw that scene in a Sainsbury's advert last night. Our tiny kitchen still had the sickly smell of last night's dinner – Iceland's fried chicken. The dregs of a cup of tea lay at the sink – it was lukewarm. Sometimes she'd leave me out Weetabix in a bowl next to the carton of milk, and a glass of fruit juice would be poured. Today, the table lay bare – only smudges of grease adorned the formica. She must have been running late this morning – she was on the day shift at the beetroot factory. I'd see her tonight with splashes of purple juice on her face and arms, like burns or large purple birthmarks. She'd promised me that when I left school she'd get me a job beside her.

'Might have to start on constant nightshift first. Just for a while. Just to get you in the door.' She said it like she was doing me a favour. I braced myself, opened the door and the rain lashed at my face.

Brian Arbuckle. It could be said that his life had not always been this bad. I remembered him from the beginning. In fact you might even say that I had been a wee pal of his. Primary School it was when he first arrived and we all adored him. Wee Brian. Daft wee Brian. Maybe you're nicer when you're younger – more tolerant. I was certainly nice to that wee bastard. I remember his skinny skittle legs trying to run for the ball – his right toe turning inwards, dragging, almost tripping him up. If you scrutinised his face – you could see some awareness that he knew that that right foot should just be behaving itself. But he'd no control. He'd just go lolloping around the pitch, teetering and tottering and threatening to trip over, and smash his teeth on the concrete. Spaz. But I was good to him, that wee spaz. I do remember that.

'Brian, pal, do you want to be in my team? Do you want to be in Sinky's team?'

He let out a big shriek. 'Yeah... me in Sinky's team... yeah'. I usually dumped him in the goals for ten minutes. The other girls loved him too – Lisa and Tracey used to play houses with him – had Brian as the baby. He loved it. He sat on the bench with his wee face looking up like a buttercup, as they brushed his yellow hair. He would do anything you told him. In our own way, we loved him. He didn't know what was coming to him back then.

I don't know exactly when it happened – round about second year of Secondary I think – but Wee Brian got big and Wee Brian got fat. All his cuteness just vanished. His face now had clusters of mini volcanoes – each one the size of a pinhead, frequently erupting thick white pus. The spots on his chin sprouted straw coloured hair to match the hair on his head. The hair on his head... what had happened to that? Gone were the days when it smelt sweet as strawberries; shiny and soft; bouncing gently as he did his Brian lollop around the field. He had attempted to style it, manipulating it with some kind of gluey gunge to spike upwards and outwards so that his head looked like a round medieval weapon. Someone should have told him how stupid he looked and maybe nothing would have happened. Instead he seemed to take pride in it.

'Sinky, you like Brian's hair? Awesome, eh?' and he tried to high-five me.

'Awww Brian, your hair is fucking fantastic,' I said, and I looked at Lisa and gave her a wink before giving him a high-five with one hand and ruffling his hair wildly with my other.

'You are such a badass sista' Lisa giggled. Brian stood there looking bewildered.

'Lisa you like Brian's hair?' He hadn't a clue. Lisa and I laughed, and Brian joined in. He liked to laugh.

'What do you think he actually uses in his hair?' asked Lisa.

'I, seriously, have no idea... hairspray? Glue? Gel? Cement? A combo?' That was the day when we first got the idea of setting wee Brian on fire – whooooosh – up in orange flames – his brittle hair first. A Beavis and Butthead classic.

As I headed towards the school, I saw Lisa on the park bench having a fag with Jen.

'Hey crash the hash – bags seconds.' I snatched the fag out Lisa's fingers as she practised blowing smoke rings up in the air, coughing and spluttering in her attempt. 'You complete arsehole,' Jen and I were doubled over. Jen was snorting – she always did this when she laughed. 'Trying to look all Audrey Hepburn and look what happens.' It occurred to me that Lisa might have told Jen about the plan. Jen was a good laugh. It might be fun to have someone else involved. I caught Lisa's eye 'Got it?'

'Sure have, dahling' She paraded the silver zippo lighter up in the air and it dazzled sharply.

'Sweet.' I said. 'And now for my next trick...' I pulled the can of Harmony hairspray from my pocket.

Jen had perked up interest 'What you lassies up to?'

'Here's a clue. Witness the scene before you: "The Interesting Combustion of the Straw Haired Boy: Brian." Whoosh and off he will go. You can record it on your phone'.

'No worries' said Jen grinning. Now we were armed with our circus equipment:

'One Zippo lighter - check; one aerosol can of Harmony hairspray – check; one

Samsung' – I had a quick glance – 'Galaxy, to record for prosperity by our one and only gifted photographer... Jen Murdoch... take a bow, hen.' Jen laugh-snorted and took an elaborate bow.

We moved as a small convoy towards the school.

We found him wandering himself, out beyond the playing fields, staring at the ground, as if searching for something lost.

'Hey Brian,' we jostled each other, running towards him, laughing and gasping with the cold morning air, and the excitement of it all.

He looked up like a forlorn dog.

'What you up to, Brian, my good man?' I put my arm around his shoulders.

'I'm sorting the snails Sinky, so they won't get lonely...putting them into families.' The daftie had been searching for snail shells to form a circle. 'Look Sinky'. He held up a particularly large tan coloured snail shell for me to inspect. 'This snail is like me – it's the king of the snails – that's what my mum says about me – that I'm royalty – that I'm the Kiiiing of the house' He laughed. 'Even more than dad.' He said it with pride. He said it with conviction.

I snatched 'King' snail from his hand, threw it onto the grass and ground the shell down, enjoying the crunch. I lifted up the sole of my shoe to show the grey snail slime to Lisa and Jen.

'Oh, soooo gross' Lisa made dry heaving sounds.

I smeared the mashed snail body onto the grass in long sweeps. Brian just stared.

'Hey Brian, my wise old owl. I know where there are many snails... more snails than you can dream of, Brian my pal... about three times the size of that king snail, Brian.' He looked bewildered. I held out my palm towards him. 'Look at Sinky's hand, Brian. I know where you can find snails that size.' And that's how we got Brian into the girl's toilets.

His mind was so caught up in snail paradise that he gave no resistance. We entered in silence. It lay on the other side of the playing field, adjacent to the woods and was rarely used and rarely cleaned. Dead brown leaves, blown in by the wind, lay scattered around, and only the grey sky shed a dim light in the room. It did not smell of piss but of earth and dampness – but most of all, it reeked of abandonment. There were no laughing school children here. Brian, for all his daftness, must have sensed that something wasn't quite right as he began to slink towards the door.

'Whoaaah, buddy, where do you think you're off to?' I grabbed his arm and pulled him towards the mirror. 'Look Brian. Look. Your hair needs fixed.'

He stared at himself in the mirror. Transfixed. I looked at Jen and Lisa who stood behind me watching, and I gave them the wink. I felt the chill of the tin in my hand and whipped it out of my pocket.

'Let Sinky help you Brian.' I held him with one arm from behind, and began saturating his hair with spray. The air was immediately filled with a thick perfume smell. I heard the zippo clink open, and from the corner of my eye, saw the blue flame quiver then light up, as Lisa moved in to torch him. In the mirror, I saw Jen with the Samsung and Brian's hair... Brian's hair sizzling orange and yellow wavering flames. He was a cartoon kid, and I whooped like a warrior with the success of it. Jen was predictably snort-laughing, although holding the phone steady. Lisa high-fived me. 'Good job sista.'

He stood paralysed. Small whimpering noises seemed to be making their way up from deep inside him. I wondered how many likes it would get on Youtube. I imagined the mark it would leave – a mark like beetroot; a burning birthmark.

Out the back of the flat

Laura Tansley

The shadow of something falls from a height and I think for a second –
what if it's a body part or worse a broken chimney descending to end me?

I worry about littering then, for a while, and wonder why someone would throw a fig
from their window, it being (on reflection) the size of a small piece of fruit.

I don't bother to find out; if it's something of value, something someone's lost
(a plant pot, the plot – once there was a single flip flop in our front garden.
Such madness), then I'm sure a sign will be put up in the close:

Don't drop anything; get a (firm) grip; take your trash to the tip.

Craning up at buildings the awkward angles of
birds and planes fall from the sky like a mirror tipping
leaving white trails of condensation and uric acid along my centre axis.

A clod of roofmoss dislodged by a gull lands in the grass
dead as a dormouse and I think

Dear Neighbours,
~~*Will my tomato plant grow here?*~~
~~*Do you think my tomato plant will flower here?*~~
Do you think my tomato plant will be happy here?

Out the back it's a real sun trap so as long as people stop throwing themselves from elevations
this thing will bear fruit.

Banton to Govan

John Boursnell

1. [Banton 11.10am]

Blue pipe
green crisp packet
cream burger carton
red water
Mare's Tail
radio, dog walker.

Lambs, barbed wire
a clumsy vault
drill sounds, Easter time
low flying crows
27 bus
though we came on the 24.

4.

We lose the river under a field
disappearing into a larger pipe
with a grill in front
there is a small amount of scum on the surface
the sort that just accumulates
on slow field edge water
there is a pair of shoes on the side
a corrugated plastic pipe drips red water into the stream
jetplane
biplane.

5. [*Canal 12.08pm*]

First pebbly drop,
river still only a few feet or less across
bank filled with Gunnera
'invasive'
there are bees
and pylons in the valley.

We reach the canal
'Jakob! stand your bike up!
can you tell Jakob to stand his bike up?'
our first buzzard, gently swooping
on the other side of the road
speeding cyclists
some in summer clothes
some geared up
all tubes for water and
vests that look bullet proof.

15. [*Two bridges*]

The first
old stone, two spans
one arch emptying now
into a browning pool
blue glass
slag
melted material
fish jump
rusting pipes falling off the side
a failure to successfully retrofit
spewing dead cables.

The second
concrete, rust, industrial
hidden banks
dog prints
some quite large
muffled, abstracted, distanced sound
fishing line
a tiny, tiny shell at my feet
unexpected
a bit of bone
bicycle racks
on the path down
a box of fireworks.

45.

We are
too high to collect water
too wide to record in a sheltered spot
eating an eel
a Van Vanette Drill
a site office
an overflowing bin
a no parking zone
washing our beaks
a crow on a lamppost
a potential development site
we are improving the image of construction.
we could be home by now.

Girl Unknown

Gillian Mellor

The book, published by Panther
is James Bond in Ian Fleming's
Goldfinger. On the cover she sits
upon a model of an automatic
9mm pistol designed by David
Collins and Floris van den Broecke.
Next to an Asprey's champagne
bucket she is holding an Asprey's
golden goblet. She wears jewellrey
by Hooper Bolton. Her photograph
was taken by Beverley le Barrow.

if you write poetry and do not like conversation

Alison Whitelock

what you can do is you can tell people at parties
that you write poetry and what that means is the people
at the parties will not know what to say to you
if they do say something mostly it will be that they do not like poetry
but because you are at a party you must make conversation
so you will say to them to not like poetry is to say
you do not like one of your ears or your right kidney
or seeing the frost curl and rise at dawn to lick your world silver
sometimes when you tell people you write poetry
what they will understand is that you stare out of the window
for too many hours and wear a cravat and smoke cigarettes
in a long cigarette holder and that you do not do anything
of any real value because you do not earn any money
from doing this thing what they will also understand
is because you write poetry you must be a poet
but they will not understand the act of writing
poetry does not necessarily make you a poet
if you try to explain this to them they will have to excuse
themselves and go to the kitchen to top up their sparkling
lambruscos because they think it is champagne
then the next person who comes will also ask you
what you do and you will say the poetry thing again
and they will ask you why you write poetry
and you will say because scottish heather flourishes
in the harshest of spots like the cracks of rocks
where there's no love and still it survives
and they will not know what you are talking
about and will think that sometimes you wear smocks
and puffy sleeves and only ever write things about tulip
petals and emerald fields and new born lambs, etc.
and sometimes they will ask you how long it takes
to write a poem and you will tell them one week or fifty
two it depends and the waiter will come around

with the platter of vol-au-vents and the blinis
topped with smoked salmon and an inch of crème fraîche
with the sprig of green dill planted like a baby christmas
tree knee deep in snow and this will be the perfect moment
for them to move away to the kitchen and top up their sparklings
too and finally you will be left alone only
you are never really alone because you will always
have your bag filled with the notebooks and the backs
of napkins and the gaggles of pens and when the party
is over your notes will say things like–

1. google blini ingredients
2. sparkling lambrusco is not champagne
3. writing poetry does not make you a poet any more
   than not killing an ant will make you a buddhist

and you will be satisfied you went to the party
and that you tried to make conversation but you decide
you will not go to the parties of the future
and you will not hate the people for not loving
poetry in the way that you love it
sure there was a time you hated poetry too

Tintinnabulation

Chin Li

I

Tintinnabulation. 'Tin – tin – nab – u – la – tion...'

    This, a mouthful of a word, I hadn't come across until ten, perhaps twelve (or was it fifteen?) years ago. I was in my twenties then. He taught me this long, undulating word, casually, with his characteristic, dismissive wave of his left hand, 'It means bells.' Just that. He didn't do small talk. (Did he talk more to *her?*) But even his gestures enchanted me.

    There was more to the word though. *Tintinnabulation: the Voice of a New Theology.* His one and only published work. Took him years to write. I'm still not sure what it is about. There are chapters on angels and bell-ringers; and, intriguingly, the final chapter has the title *The Booming Christ.* The book got poor reviews: nobody understood what he was saying. He tried, but never managed to publish anything else. All this I only discovered much later.

    Change-ringing – that was his passion. He was a fanatical bell-ringer in his youth. He once said to me that church bells were sacred and bell-ringing was a sacrament as important as the Eucharist. I didn't know what he meant, but I'm sure he did say that to me. I am sure.

    Now I hate church bells: can't stand their peals of laughter mocking me!

    When he first arrived at the diocesan house where the priests lived, the church bells were ringing for the noonday *Angelus.* From the window of the office, I saw him standing there in the forecourt, eyes shut, arms raised and body swaying slightly, as if in a trance. My heart missed a beat, and my face went bright red – fortunately there was nobody else in the office. I knew there and then I had fallen madly in love. When I found out he was celebrating Mass the following evening, I made sure I was sitting right at the front. I was trembling the whole time, unable to sit still. I felt bad that God wasn't on my mind, but the sense of guilt didn't stop the thrill of secret excitement rushing through my body.

    'May the grace of God, the love of Christ and the fellowship of the Holy Ghost be with you all...' His voice boomed. With open arms, he stared at a point in space above the congregation: his eyes intense and blazing. I was mesmerised. How I wished he would look at me and notice I was there.

    Later on that evening I prayed fervently, trying desperately to coax God into giving me a sign that he was a gift from Him.

    A few days later I was introduced to him properly. He needed somebody to type up a manuscript, and as the office wasn't busy, I was asked to do it. He gave me a copy of *Tintinnabulation* so I could follow its elaborate format. And then he handed me a bundle of papers, his hand-written draft of the first chapter of another book, with the title page simply marked *GMP.*

    Although he was 43 (how did I find out?), he still retained a haunting boyish beauty... I could cry, even now, thinking about it.

II

One day, we were working on the *GMP* draft well into the evening. I didn't know what I was typing – not only because of the strangeness of the content (a lot about all human embryos starting off as female), but also because my mind wasn't working properly. I could read all his words, and my fingers could transcribe them more or less accurately on to the computer, but their meaning was too dense for me to grasp. I was taken hostage by his sheer presence, as he paced up and down the room reading the printout, mumbling to himself.

    When he came to our diocese, there wasn't any space for him in the priests' quarters upstairs; and so he took the small study at the back on the ground floor, where a single bed was made up for him. The church office was at the front of the house, and my desk was next to a large bay window. Looking out of that window and seeing him arrive on the first day had sealed my fate.

    How I wish his manuscript would never end! How I wish I could serve him like a true disciple! His handwriting was peculiar, and his prose tortuous, with many clauses in each sentence leading to numerous labyrinths. As I was typing, I had to look out of the window every now and then to ease my eyes and to clear my mind. But I relished the challenge, willingly submitting myself to his power.

    Perhaps I was made for tragedy, as I had a premonition, right from the start, that I wouldn't be the star of the story. I was but a minor character, one that could be deleted without the plot being affected in any significant way. That knowledge hurt me deeply (and still does), and when it was confirmed, an intense loathing took possession of my heart. Of course he was the star; but I wasn't given the role of the heroine. My hatred was directed against the usurper who took my place. *She* had robbed me of what was rightfully mine; her ignorance of it did not excuse her. She didn't even know I existed.

    But I was his teacher who led him into a new mystery. His seminary education was completely devoid of love, and I'm sure he was a virgin when he first arrived at our diocese. There were three of us working in the office, and the other two women were already grandmothers. But that didn't stop them ogling him and winking at each other all the time.

    'Here, this is wrong! You should know there's a "p" in the middle of this word.' He shoved the printout under my nose. The pencil in his left hand nearly poked me in the eye. This was so sudden, and so out of my expectation that I burst into tears straight away. It was already nine o'clock, and it'd been such a long, dark evening.

    Taken aback, he sat down, speechless. After a few moments, he raised his right hand, and said in a husky voice. "Look, I'm sorry," he cleared his throat, "do you want to call it a day?" I kept my head down and didn't answer him. Tears were still streaming down my face, but I was aware that they had nothing to do with his criticism of my typing. It was the strain of being with him in the same room that did it.

He stood up, and I panicked. I didn't want him to go – my tears turned into sobs. He sat down and then abruptly stood up again. Without thinking, I rose up towards him, but in a clumsy movement knocked a pile of papers off the desk. As if choreographed by some ancient gods, we both reached out to catch the papers. Somehow he stumbled and fell, in slow motion, towards me. My arms instinctively opened to stop him, and my chest stemmed his fall. Before I knew it, I had him in a tight hug, my head on his shoulder and my lips on his neck. His body stiffened, but he didn't push me off. We stood entwined in a rather awkward position, my back straining to balance both of us and his hands limply touching my bum. I thought I was whispering "I love you, I love you..." repeatedly, but it was probably all in my head.

I can't remember how what happened next happened. There were only fragments in my mind: images of his study-bedroom with the book-lined walls swirling round *above* me, the sound of the creaking of his bed and the smell of his sweaty body - all of these conjuring up an intense sense of triumph, but also of foreboding, that had stayed with me ever since.

III

That first night was over very quickly – must have been only minutes. He was fumbling, not knowing how to position himself. Although I had a constant headache, I was guiding him wordlessly all the way. And I was still yearning for him when he finished. It was a messy, unsatisfying few minutes. But I also felt, strangely, acute elation. Ever since childhood, I had often experienced an intense ecstasy for God; that night God came to me.

He fell asleep on top of me for a while till I could no longer bear his weight. I tried to wriggle out without waking him, but he woke up immediately. He rolled out of bed, dashed to the window and drew the curtains. The room turned pitch-black, and a sudden fear overwhelmed me. As I grabbed the bedcover to hide my body, his disembodied voice drifted across the room, 'Please go now.' A hoarse voice, devoid of emotions.

I knew he was avoiding me in the following days. Then late one afternoon, he came into the office and gave me another chapter of *GMP* to type. After working in complete silence for hours, he took me to his room – and I had to hold on to him when he locked the door because the room was in total darkness. From then on, I went there nearly every night, after *GMP*. But he never let me talk when we were in his room.

Very quickly I got used to the darkness – he wouldn't switch on any light when I was there. But I found it hard to cope with the feeling of being cut off from him when his animal ferocity crushed into me and *I couldn't see his face.* I'd like to see love, or at least tenderness, in his eyes. It was only after a couple of weeks did he allow me to touch his face with my hand. He never let me kiss him on the lips. He did become more agile over time, and I consoled myself with the hope that perhaps in due course he would learn to love me as he had learned to make love to me.

I couldn't make sense of what happened subsequently: how that bitch managed to capture him. I was the one with better looks, but she became the star and I remained a dispensable extra. At the time, I could only put it down to her worldly success: she was a well-known lawyer. She'd done a great deal of legal work for the diocese, and got a lot of praise from the Bishop. Now I believe she must have been a witch – she had seduced him with black magic. It pains me so, to think what bliss could have been mine (and his) if she didn't exist.

IV

She appeared on the scene some months after he came to the diocese. He was appointed deputy chair of a new committee which was given the task of reviewing the theological education of priests, and she was asked by the Bishop to chair it. The first, and only, time I saw her was when the committee held their inaugural meeting in the library of the diocesan house. I had to serve as minute-taker because the assistant to the Bishop, who was the secretary of the committee, was unwell that day.

In the meeting, I did my best to concentrate on the discussion, but it was very difficult because shortly after it had started, I realised I had encountered a formidable enemy. She chaired the meeting with aplomb and skill. She was charming: talking and laughing as if the world was her oyster. Everybody was openly appreciative of her (only I saw her evil side). I could sense that *he* wasn't just impressed by her leadership qualities – he couldn't take his eyes off her the whole evening.

After the meeting, she asked him to stay on to discuss things further, and I was told I wasn't needed. As soon as I arrived home, I regretted not staying behind. I so desperately wanted to talk to him. It was plain that they were attracted to each other. I cried myself to sleep that night.

The following day he was nowhere to be found. No one knew where he was. I made it known that I wanted him to check the minutes of the meeting, even though I hadn't, in fact, touched the notes I took the night before. I didn't see him until the following week, when he came into the office one morning to say the committee would not hold its meetings here anymore; instead they would be held at various locations in the diocese. I tried to find out more about her in an oblique way, but he resolutely refused to even mention her name. It was a short conversation, and I was fighting back my tears. Having given me the agenda for the second meeting, he was turning to go, and I made a last-ditch attempt to detain him. I asked him, clumsily, about further chapters of *GMP* to type. *GMP* had become our bond, our password. He stopped at the door, but I couldn't see his face. It felt like a frozen frame in a movie: it couldn't have been more than a few seconds, yet it was a hiatus of a lifetime.

'I've decided to shelf the book.' He said tersely. I rose, but he was already gone. As I fell back down on my chair, a feeling of doom enveloped me. The following weeks were like one long bad dream – I tried to go to work but couldn't manage it at all. I spent most of my time lying in bed at home, drifting in and out of some nightmarish, twilight world. I knew she must have cast a spell on him. My mother was worried sick and came to stay with me for a while, but was unable to do much to help. I couldn't understand why I didn't die of grief.

V

It was weeks before I felt strong enough to return to work. I was looking for him every day, but he avoided me. He would only speak to me when there were other people around, and did so as if he wasn't sure he knew my name. My mind was in a frenzy. There were several occasions when I was nearly able to engineer an opportunity to speak to him alone, but he always managed to find a way to disappear promptly.

I felt desolate, totally destroyed. His angelic face kept appearing whenever I shut my eyes. Sleep was impossible – I lay in bed every night, half-unconscious and half-awake, my body rigid with pain. He was (and still is) my destiny, and she had so cruelly snatched him away from me.

Then one evening I couldn't stand it any longer, and decided to stay in the office after work to wait for him. I turned off the light and locked the door. The priests upstairs usually went to bed early – they were much older, and didn't seem to have any social life. The whole house became quiet and still when it was barely ten o'clock. I waited, my heart thumping hard.

He wasn't around the whole day. I secretly checked his room during my lunch break, but it was locked. My mind was racing: *What am I doing? What am I going to do?* I was tired, and my body was aching. I curled up in my chair trying to rest, and dozed off without meaning to. When I woke up later, I was dismayed to find it was already half past twelve. I wanted to catch him when he came in, but wasn't sure now if he was already back and asleep. I hesitated, not knowing what to do. *Am I going mad?* All I knew was I must talk to him.

After a few agonising moments, I unlocked the door and went into the dark corridor. I walked past the library and the dining room quietly; when I turned the corner his door came into sight, only a few paces away. I was aware of something, but had no idea what it was at first. Then it hit me hard like a thunderbolt – it was the creaking of his bed. The familiar rhythmic noise pounded my heart, and my face turned red hot instantly. In a moment of madness, I was going to barge into the room. But I stopped myself, knowing the door would be locked. I couldn't move; my hands pressing hard against the wall for support. Suddenly, without warning, came her moans. They were like murmurings at first, but became louder very quickly. I didn't know whether indeed I heard them or it was just me screaming in my head. Then a crescendo of sounds exploded inside my ears, and I turned and ran. I stumbled into the office, gasping for air. My mind was jumbled up: I knew I was crying, but couldn't hear a sound. Everything went black. But somehow I saw myself hitting her: *Die, you bitch, die!* She was laughing at me. I was sitting on top of her, pounding her chest with my fists, like a maniac...

VI

I had killed them both. That much I am sure of. But I only meant to kill her, not him. Maybe God in His mercy and infinite wisdom saw fit to take them both. He was innocent though: he was bewitched. She was the only guilty one. Of course no one knows whether he has died – he disappeared, never to be seen again. But I know in my heart that he no longer lives.

That fateful evening ended in a mess. I found myself lying on the floor of the office when I was woken up by the commotion of people running back and forth in the corridor. It was half past two in the morning. I dragged myself up and looked out of the window, careful to hide myself behind the curtain. There was an ambulance with its back doors wide open, and a police car beside it. Several people were standing there, talking in low voices. Suddenly a great fear overcame me and I quickly lay down on the floor again, my whole body shaking. *What have I done?* I held on to the legs of a chair to steady my mind, and then fainted.

When I woke up a second time, the church bells were ringing: their announcement of the new day. Six o'clock. Tintinnabulation. The house was eerily quiet. I opened the door ajar to have a peek, and saw all the lights were on even though there didn't seem to be anyone about. I felt so exhausted I just went home.

Later I phoned in sick and stayed in bed. When I returned to work a couple of days later, the other two women in the office were full of gossip but I shut myself off, saying I was still unwell. One of them left a copy of the local paper on her desk. The headline *Lawyer Died in Sex Romp with Priest* stared at me menacingly. I wasn't surprised. Apparently many people were greatly excited by the prospect of an inquest, but in the end there was to be no inquest because no foul play was found. Her doctor had confirmed that she had a long history of serious congenital heart troubles, and her liaison with a priest wasn't a crime. Somebody said the Bishop had spoken to several key people and the whole thing was quickly, and quietly, resolved.

Many months later, I received a letter from Peru. There was no signature, but I could instantly recognise his handwriting. It was a brief message: *Please kindly destroy all your files to do with GMP – this is the greatest favour you could do a dying man.* And there was a p.s. – *GMP is 'God: Mother or Paramour?' In case you wonder.*

I didn't destroy any of the files but saved them all on a memory stick (I think I did). Four and a half chapters: perhaps one day I'll complete the book for him.

One of the Good Ones

Gavin Gilmour

So this is a dilemma. I can't help but feel that it's all because of Gregor and the money I loaned him.

Maybe that's unfair. Surely he couldn't have imagined the consequences of the loan would have led us here – to this sodden garden, god knows where. No one would even contemplate putting a friend in that position knowingly, certainly not Gregor, he's a decent man.

Anyway, is that what they want to hear? I'm not really sure, it's difficult to make out exactly due to all the shouting. Sometimes I'm only catching the end of a sentence or the beginning of another. At least it's not for a lack of trying on their part though, they've been shouting very loudly for a number of minutes now, and occasionally intimately close to my face, I catch little whiffs of their breath, not dis-similar to Gregor's – a little bit odd. I am listening though, I can see their mouths are moving. I just don't have the words at hand to respond. So it's understandable that they might be irate, at least I can understand it.

If someone were to walk in blind to this situation, without knowing all of the background details then yes, I imagine it would look quite worrying: me standing in the corner of a suburban back garden whilst a young woman and her semi-naked partner – I presume it's her partner – lurch at me shouting obscenities (from what I can make out).

The dilemma is two-fold – firstly, its very difficult to compose yourself and coherently voice a testimony of defence whilst being verbally intimidated, and secondly, by describing the origin to the chain of events that led to this scenario and therefore attempt to answer the central question the screaming woman and her partner have just asked, that being, 'What are you doing in our back garden?' responding with details about the loan to Gregor three months ago will be unlikely to placate their aggressive demand for answers.

As I seem to be struggling to find a reasonable argument with which to counter their inquisition, I have sympathy for them. My sudden appearance scrambling over their garden fence would frighten most level headed people. This was a dilemma I had brought to their door on a cold and bitter morning in early February. They didn't ask for it and from their response I can see that they are not entirely happy to receive it. But here it is none the less. If I could change it, I would. That the benefit of hindsight should come to me now is just a reflection of my poor judgement over the past few months. To be honest – and if I can claim to be anything at all, I pray that at very least, I am honest – I feel guilty implicating Gregor in this shoddy state of affairs at all. But if the portly woman wearing a baby pink dressing gown and smeared makeup truly wants to know what I'm doing here then I have to start with Gregor and the two hundred pounds I loaned him.

If I can gather my thoughts and explain from there the series of mundane and unlikely events that have led to this wholly unnecessary scene then hopefully her boyfriend can be encouraged to lower the Irn-Bru bottle he grips in his hand and pop back inside to put some clothes on. Not that his pale, skinny and tattoo-marked frame is offensive to me but I just imagine wearing only your boxer shorts in such freezing temperatures cannot be pleasant. I've caused enough of a stir to his day to then be the cause of inflicting a nasty cold upon his probably already weakened immune system – his wiry stature and pallid complexion led me to infer his immunity may be weak. A diet of sugary Irn-Bru also won't be helping him.

Of course, if this spitting fury of a man and his fraught partner are the totem at the top of my metaphorical iceberg then Gregor is the icy cold foundation. So by default you could argue that the obvious action to have reversed, if possible, would be *not* to have loaned the money to Gregor. A relatively easy conclusion to come to and goodness me, I wish I had been endowed with this critical foresight at the time. Though if we were all given fair warning to the cause and effect nature that even our simplest of actions might trigger then I doubt we would ever make firm choices at all. We would be frozen by the intricate and complex paths that lay before any decision, no matter how apparently inconsequential. Just thinking about it makes me anxious.

But Gregor is a decent man, one of the good ones. He has a tendency to openly disregard his attention to personal hygiene, but that's just part of what makes Gregor, Gregor, I suppose? The smell. And the funny breath, not necessarily bad breath, just a little bit odd – a stale sweet smell, the kind you notice when someone drinks tea straight after smoking a cigarette. Although Gregor doesn't smoke.

He has an irrepressible personality – he can be very convincing. Not that I needed to be convinced, in fact there was very little persuasion required on his part. He had held my gaze, head raised, hands in his pockets, a slightly hunched look about the shoulders, his request direct and purposeful.

'I'm gonna need to borrow some money Ed.'

He followed this with a sort of bobbing head nod like his neck had become elastic and loose whilst releasing air through his nostrils, as if he were simultaneously reaffirming his statement and acknowledging the undercurrent of tension.

In the few seconds of silence that followed I tried to assess whether or not he was being serious, Gregor says what he thinks, without filtering anything, a trait I admire but it still catches you off-guard at times.

'Uh-huh. Okay are you –

'Two hundred quid. It's a fantastic opportunity. Fantastic. Be stupid to let this one go, stupid.'

'Oh really, so what's the –

'Whippets.'

I was again taken off-guard.

'Whippets?'

'Whippets.'

'Oh. Right, so what do you –

'What I'm saying to you is that I've been given a fantastic opportunity, I mean, a *truly fantastic* opportunity to become involved in something here, something I'd be totally stupid to turn down.'

'...an opportunity –'

'a fantastic opportunity.'

'– involving –'

'I mean really Ed, I'd be an idiot to turn this down.'

'– involving whippets?'

'Whippets, yes.'

'The breed of dog?'

'Yes, Whippets.'

So the thought has not escaped me that this could very easily have been the moment to challenge Gregor and change the course of events to follow; ask him what his intentions were with whippets and why he really needed the money, but that would have inferred a presumption of doubt upon his 'fantastic opportunity' and I think that would be unfair on Gregor, like I say, he's persuasive.

Quiet and confident, Gregor was always more ambitious. His mum though, was very strict. When we were nine he once took some rope from their garage to make a swing. She walked in to collect something from their outside freezer and caught him lifting it from under a workbench. She then proceeded to knee him in the behind repeatedly. I watched on in horror – frozen by the explosion of fury and violence she had released on him. The shame of silently witnessing it and Gregor's subsequent hysterical tears would stay with me for some time afterwards. I had only known him a short while then – we had hired Gregor's mum as a cleaner and after getting to know her (or not, I felt) my mum asked her if she could take me after school for a few hours twice a week as she worked part time on those days and wouldn't finish till later. Having only been playmates a handful of times at school, it took a week or so before Gregor and I got used to the arrangement. After a mutual acknowledgment that we may have different backgrounds and homes of different size, smell and look, we soon became good friends.

'This old boy up at the farm is breeding them.'

Gregor's head flicked back to indicate the direction of the farm.

'Mr McLean?'

'He's breeding them and he's offered me an investment opportunity.'

It's at this moment I had become acutely aware of our exposure to the neighbours – I had only just answered the door to Gregor and after a very brief exchange of pleasantries, he had launched into his appeal for the loan. I acknowledged my oversight of manners and ushered him into the house. Without any response he walked straight in but stopped sharply at the foot of my staircase, barely over the threshold of the front door, and turned to face me, hands still in his pockets.

As I closed the door behind us, I tried to process the information he had given me.

'So, this is an investment to breed whippets?'

'In a way – it allows access to the market, capitalising on the current surge in demand. And some neat little kickbacks.'

He smirked and did his nodding head thing again. Due to Gregor's position at the foot of my stairs I found myself unable to manoeuvre around him and therefore caged into my cramped vestibule. Scanning my surroundings for a physical point to lean on and realising there wasn't one, I somewhat awkwardly placed my palms on my lower back, forcing my hips forward like a camp bullfighter taunting his adversary but without the conviction. I immediately crossed my arms instead, the go-to gesture for the defensive passive aggressive.

'Right, well that sounds like a really interesting... you know, it sounds like you've done some research and it could be, you know—'

'An opportunity.'

'Well, yes, that's what it sounds like.'

'A fantastic opportunity.'

'Sure. If that's what –'

'You know Ed I had a feeling you'd be the right person for this, I really did, you get it, you just get it, don't you?'

I snorted out a flattered little guffaw and then released my crossed arms to let my hands sit casually on my hips.

'Well I don't know about that, I'm just... so you considered others?'

'For about a nano-second and even then it was a wasted nano-second as you were clearly the man to come to.'

'Oh. That's... really kind of you Gregor.'

'Yeah. So lets do this, lets do business. The sooner I can get this to Mr McLean the better, make hay as they say.'

'Make hay? Oh, yes of course, when the sun shines.'

'Sure. If the sun shines too then great, bonus. I like that Ed, Christ, I knew you were my man for this.'

'Indeed. So do you have an idea what the two hundred pounds will be invested in or –

'Tell you what mate, its only fair, this should be a joint investment, I like to think I'm a decent man, this is a fantastic opportunity and fantastic opportunities don't come along everyday. Yes, business is a brutal and unforgiving world Ed, but Christ it needn't be, yeah? So lets do this, lets go fifty-fifty. You want in? Be stupid to turn this down Ed.'

'Oh... really?'

'Absolutely, this is as sure a thing as I've ever seen mate – its golden. We'll make quadruple our investment at least. I'll pay you back the hundred quid and you get whatever else on top. It's a win-win for you my friend.'

I'm still amazed at the speed with which I was enticed into a situation that was to snowball out of control, like an unwieldy Catherine wheel spinning dangerously off its base, attacking its audience, namely me. Like any decision you may come to regret, the memory of the act itself seems so slight and sudden that you can barely discern that such a thing had happened at all.

Of course, this is all digression, full of excuses and reapportioning of blame. Even if I were to pitifully argue that Gregor had wilfully and possibly even deceptively sold me a deal that involved illegal activities with whippets, I would still be denying the true responsibilities that lay solely at my feet.

I said yes. I was weak. I was eager to please. I was foolish. I bit. I was had. Now Gregor had me, and my two hundred pounds sterling.

Later that night I sat in my kitchen and drank a cup of tea. I remember it distinctly. I must have been deep in thought as it was only when the timer clicked the switch of the table lamp that sat on my sideboard, illuminating the corner of the room, that I realised I had been sitting in the gloom, the half mug of tea gone cold. Reminiscing about times gone past.

When I was little, eight years old maybe, I recall asking my mother while she was driving us home from the city what she thought of a friend of mine at the time – I can't remember whom, but not Gregor – Alistair Grimmer I think. We had fallen out over something only eight year olds can fall out over, friendships seemed so fragile at that age. Mum always said I was very sensitive. Anyway, she responded curtly and with an impatience that made me realise I was being petty, overbearing even.

'Don't be so stupid Edward. I have no idea!'

When I look back and think about that gloomy kitchen on that evening – time passing me by, the silence within it only broken by the dull click of the light, I can hear those clipped words from my mother echoing in my mind.

*

I didn't hear from Gregor again for a number of weeks, I presumed he was busy developing our investment opportunity – I hoped he was seeing some of those nice little kickbacks he talked about, even if I wasn't.

The doorbell rang just as I was halfway through eating a Lorne sausage roll, the heavy, floury bread sticking to the roof of my mouth as I opened the door and tried to utter some welcoming platitude.

'... oh, hi Gregor.' I gulped down the doughy roll.

'Time to see the fruits of your labour Ed.'

'What's that now?' I fished some of the roll from my teeth.

'Well not so much labour I suppose – wrong words – what I mean to say is the hay has been made.'

Behind Gregor a rusty and bruised looking van sat idling on the street. I could see a young boy with a shorn head sitting on the passenger seat watching me with his mouth slightly ajar, expressionless.

'Oh, is that your son with you Gregor? Does he want to come –'

'The boy's fine. Not a people person. No time to come in Ed. Do you want to see where your money has gone?'

I did. In fact, as soon as I had opened the door to Gregor I was anxious to discover what had come of the two hundred pounds.

'Well, sure – I'd be delighted to.'

'Good. Grab your jacket and jump in the van.'

Sitting next to Gregor's son, Gregor Jnr, for the short fifteen-minute drive up to the field next to Mr Mclean's farm confirmed to me that Gregor Snr was indeed correct in his sweeping and conclusive analysis of his son's personality: the boy appeared not to be a people person.

By the time we arrived and Gregor had opened the back doors of the battered van to reveal the caged whippets, I was of the mind that this was not looking to be the type of investment I might have hoped for. Gregor jumped into the back of the van, pushing a cardboard box towards his son who collected it and sat it down on the damp grass of the field.

'Here they are Ed! Good looking dogs eh?'

I had caught a glimpse of the contents of the cardboard box as the boy passed me; dog leads, knives, a small video camera and a blood stained, pockmarked cricket bat. A feeling of regret seemed to wash over me and I suppose it was at this point that I knew things had taken a turn for the worse.

'Sure, what are you planning on –'

'Fa's this boy?'

I turned and saw Mr McLean approaching holding his shepherd's crook. I'd seen Mr McLean many times walking with his sheep dogs. I used to go to school with his son, Eric, but Mr McLean would have no recollection of me I'm sure. He once arrived at a school sports day in his tractor and boiler suit, covered in filth; poor Eric never did live that one down.

I could see the hares over his shoulder, at the top of the field. They sat and ate near the dry stone dyke that separated the grass field from the pine trees that sat up on the ridge. Their numbers were many but still they seemed too far away from us to be in danger.

'Sandy, meet Ed – Ed this is Sandy McLean.' Gregor had jumped out of the van and taken a lead from the cardboard box.

'Riddee ti see some hoorin fast dugs Ed?'

Mr McLean bashed his crook against one of the cages – inside a gaunt looking whippet barked and whined. Its streamlined face bared a frothing mouth and teeth.

Gregor looked delighted with himself, genuinely proud and eager to share his business venture with me.

'See, with whippets, you can let them course and race and that brings an audience with cash and blah, blah, blah… all well and good but now things have changed. Now there's a whole other audience out there – a massive audience – ready to pay more! Gregor! Camera!'

Gregor Jnr appeared from behind me with the mini video camera, lifting it up in his palm like he was holding aloft a winning trophy, something to behold.

'There's your investment my friend! There it is – video, the internet. Have you any idea how popular whippets are on the internet?'

'Streamin. It's a the streamin.' Added Mr McLean unconvincingly.

The situation was rapidly becoming apparent. My good faith in Gregor's use of the loan money and this business opportunity seemed to be very much misplaced. I often have a recurring nightmare in which I'm back at school sitting an important exam and quickly realise that I'm completely underprepared – I haven't revised the subject. It was this same fear and confusion that gripped me in the field next to Mr McLean's farm. I have little knowledge about whippets and racing them, I know even less about hare coursing and filming it, except of course, that it's illegal.

'Wait till you see this Ed, honestly, what an opportunity this –

Gregor was opening the cage door as he said this, I'm not sure if he finished his sentence or not but the whippet was on Mr McLean in a matter of seconds. It jumped up onto his chest, snarling, sending Mr McLean reeling backwards. I saw Gregor Jnr screaming and swinging the cricket bat at the dog, seemingly having no effect.

Then we heard the sirens.

Everything became imbued with panic and confusion. I saw the boy's contorted face look up from the whippet attacking Mr McLean, whose face was now bloody.

'Da! Pigs are here again!'

But Gregor was already in the van, blue smoke from its exhaust, wheels spinning in the grassy turf.

The boy turned and ran, still holding the cricket bat. The whippet bolted after him.

I ran too. And kept running. I didn't look back. I could hear the sirens and shouting fade behind me, just the sound of blood pumping through my head as my limbs strained violently, desperately.

I ran through ditches, over walls, fences, across tarmac, down lanes and pavements. My head was clear; I thought of nothing, an empty vessel being carried by strained muscle.

The burning fire in my chest could take no more and I came to rest eventually. Then I vomited. I slid down to my knees and noticed I was making noises I've never made before, guttural, animal noises.

I have no idea how long I was kneeling there. Could have been hours. I looked up and they were standing there, the baby pink dressing gown and the semi-naked man, shouting. I couldn't explain it. They looked like a grotesque painting come alive, and still they shouted. It was then that I began to laugh, bile drooling from my mouth. I laughed and laughed until I felt the urge to run again, to just keep running.

The Wiss tae be a Reid Indian

Franz Kafka

(translated by *Thomas Clark*)

Ach, tae be an Indian, an gleg on a skelpin horse, heeldin intae the wund as ye're dinnelt ower the scudderin grund again an again; tae cast aside yer spurs, for ye needit nae spurs, an thraw awa the reins, for ye needit nae reins, an tae hairdly see the laund aheid as a smuithly shorn muir afore the heid an hause o yer horse had mizzelt awa.

The Truth Aboot Sancho Panza

Franz Kafka

(translated by *Thomas Clark*)

Sancho Panza – wha, bi the wey, niver blowstit aboot it – managed, ower the years, throu primin it wi auld yairns o knichts an romance, tae sae sinder hissel fae his deil, wha he later gied the name o Don Quixote, that this deil thereby set gallusly oot on the maist capernoitit anterins which, for the want o a predetermined object (which shoud o been Sancho Panza himsel) hurtit naebody. A free man, Sancho Panza follaed Don Quixote philosophically on his adventurs, mebbes oot o a certaint mense o responsibeelity, and had oot o him a great deal o instructiounal enterteenment until the end o his days.

Unsicht

James Robertson

(A free translation of 'L'Aveugle' by *Guy de Maupassant*)

Whit is it, in the spring, that maks that first blink o sun sae braw? When that licht faws on ye, dae ye no jist full up wi the sense that life is guid? The sky's aw blue, the land green, the hooses white; and yer een sook in aw thae colours and yer lugs aw the soonds o life, and yer sowl itsel taks wing like a laverock. And yer haill ingyne is kittled up: ye want tae dance, tae run, tae sing, there's a lichtsomeness in ye, a waarmth and tenderness that spreids oot tae awbody. Ye feel ye could gie the sun itsel a kiss and a smoorich.

But whit aboot the blin men? Whit dae they feel? They staun as they aye dae at the mooths o closes, their faces steekit in ayebidin nicht. They're lown and passive in the mids o aw this new energy, and they're aye sootherin their dugs as if they dinna quite ken why the beasts should be sae fretfu and yivverie.

When they gang hame at the day's end, mibbe cleekin on tae the airm o a wee brither or sister that's been sent tae convoy them, if the bairn says, 'Whit a braw day it's been!' they say, 'Aye, I thocht it must be. Luath widna bide still for a meenit.'

I'm gaun tae tell ye aboot yin o these sichtless men, whase life wis yin o the sairest trauchles ye could ever imagine.

A peasant he wis, a fermer's laddie oot awa frae the city. Sae lang as his faither and mither were alive, he didna fair ower badly: aw he'd tae thole wis his unsicht. But, sune as the auld folk dee'd, that's when the horror begun for him. He wis taen in by a sister, on a ferm whaur awbody treated him like a scroonger for eatin the breid that ithers had tchauved tae provide. Ilka meal wis begrudgit him; they cried him an eejit and a wastrel; and even though his guid-brither had swicked him o his pairt o the heritance, they were sweer tae gie him even a bowlie o broth, and even then ainly jist eneuch tae keep him frae stervin.

His face wis geyan gash, and his twa muckle een were white as kirk wafers; and he tholed aw the insults wi a siccar mooth and a stieve face, sae that naebody could tell if he felt them. He'd never kent muckle kindness: even his ain mither had aye been sherp wi him, no shawin him ony real luve; for if a man canna dae his share o the wark in the fields whit uiss is he? Peasant folk spare nae sentiment on sic maitters. They admire the hens in the yaird, that hae a peckin order and whiles kill aff the weakest amang them, for the guid o the tribe.

Efter he'd had his broth, he'd awa and sit oot at the door in simmer, in at the lum in winter, and he widna shift tae the forenicht. He widna move, he widna speak; but aye the blinnerin lids o his een wid be flichterin ower the whiteness ablow. Whit wis he thinkin? Did he hae ony sense at aw whit his life wis aboot? Naebody could be fashed tae fin oot.

That wis hoo it wis for a hantle years. But the fact that he couldna dae ocht, as weel as the fact that naethin seemed tae pit him up nor doon, turned his faimly against him. He became the butt o their gecks and jamphs, a kind o gowk-mairtyr, a prap for whitiver they ettled tae fling at him.

There wis nae limit tae the cruelties that his unsicht lowsed in them. In order tae recompense themsels for whit he ate, they made his meals intae gemmes: oors o agony for him, oors o pleisure for the neebors.

Folk frae the nearhaun clachans cam by tae jine in the fun; the wurd gaed frae door tae door, and the ferm kitchen wis fair chokit wi bodies ilka day. Whiles a cat or a dug wid be pit on the table, in front o the bowl that he wis aboot tae tak his soup frae. The beast's ain ingyne tellt it that the man couldna see, and it wid sleekitly draw near, makkin nae soond, and cannily lap at the soup; and if an unco lood plash o its tung alerted the puir deil, it wid wicely retreat in order tae jouk the wild skelp that he'd mak at it wi his spune.

Syne there wid be hootin and dunchin and rampin o bitts frae the onlookers reenged the lenth o the waw. And himsel, athoot a word, wid stert tae eat yince mair wi his richt haun, while wi his left airm he tried tae guaird and bield his plate.

At ither times they pit corks in his soup, dauds o widd, leaves and girss; even keech, that crottled awa sae he couldna pick it oot.

Syne they wearied o their ploys; and the guid-brither, mad that he wis ayewis haein tae feed the craitur, took tae batterin him, lounderin him athoot mercy and lauchin at his uissless efforts tae jouk the blaws or hit back. Sae this wis the new gemme: the gemme o skelps – blin man's buff wi a real blin man. The ploomen, the orraman and the kitchen lassies wid pit their hauns richt in at his face, and this stertit the blinnerin movement o his ee-lids. He didna ken whaur the nixt scud or sclaff wid come frae, and had tae keep his airms streetched oot aw the time tae fend aff their shots at him.

Efter aw this, they gart him beg. They set him oot at the roadside on mercat days, and whenever he heard a body gang past or the rackle o a coach, he wis tae haud oot his bunnet and caw, 'Spare ony chynge, please?'

But fermers are no rife wi their siller, and for haill weeks he didna bring hame a bawbee.

Sae at last wis unyokit upon him a hatred that wis athoot ony trace o pity. And this brings me tae the mainner o his daith.

It wis winter, and the grund wis happit ower wi snaw, and it froze wi a dour and terrible hardness. His guid-brither, ae mornin, took him a lang gait tae a main road, and left him tae cadge frae onybody that micht pass by. He left him there aw day, but when he gaed back in the gloamin he said he wisna able tae find him. 'Ach, but we'll no fash,' he said. 'Somebody'll hae taen him in because he wis cauld. He's aye been guid at makkin folk feel sorry for him! He'll turn up the morn's morn for his soup, see if he disna.'

But the morn's morn, he didna kythe.

I doot the wey it happened wis this. Efter waitin for oors, grippit ticht wi the cauld, and feelin himsel shuttin doon and daith hotchin aboot him, the blin man wid hae begun tae walk. No able tae feel the road, which wis unner a scruif o ice, he'd hae waunered aw weys, stoitin and staucherin, pitchin intae sheuchs and sclimmin back oot, gettin himsel on his feet, settin aff yince mair, aye haudin forrit, aye gettin naewhaur, aye silent in the toom silence aw roonaboot him, as he socht a hoose or ony kind o bield for the nicht.

But there wis nane, and bit by bit the lourdness o the snaw invadit him, and his dwaiblie legs couldna cairry him ony further, and he sat doon in the middle o a field. And he didna rise again.

The bonnie white flichans fell athoot cease. Sune his shilpit body wis smoorit wi the aye-deepenin snaw; and there wis naethin tae tell whaur the body lay.

For a haill eicht days his faimly made a muckle shaw o speirin efter him and lookin for him. They even grat for him.

It wis a roch, dour winter and the thaw wis lang in comin. But, ae Sunday, on their wey tae kirk, the fermers saw a muckle flock o craws turnin and hingin ower a particlar field, drappin doon like a black plump o rain, syne risin again, drappin and risin, and ayewis returnin tae the same spot.

The week efter they were aye there, thae thrawn, dreich birds, a great clood o them that seemed tae hae gaithered frae aw the airts; and they drappit doon wi muckle skreichs intae the skinklin snaw, makkin a weird pattern o black tashes upon it, like the pattern o a kaleidoscope ainly wi nae colours.

A laddie gaed ower tae see whit they were aboot, and fund whit remained o the body o the blin man, hauf-eaten. His sichtless een were awready awa, pykit oot by the lang, sherp nebs o the hungry craws.

And I can never feel yince mair the braw bricht days o spring, athoot sparin a thocht for that puir freenless sowl. Nor can I pit frae my mind whit his faimly uissed tae say: that his life had been that sad and sair on accoont o his unsicht, that, awfie though it wis tae think on it, his daith wis a mercy and a solace tae awbody that had kent him.

The Elderly Scientist

Sally Evans

That's Wittgenstein, I say to the elderly scientist,
pointing to a dark photo in the book he has opened.
The elderly scientist likes me. He calls me 'dear'.
In Wittgenstein we have a mutual friend.
The elderly scientist shows me a picture of a horse.
I'm going to ride him in Nederlands, he says.
I don't jump him any more.

In our homes we show ourselves inside out,
allowing our friends to see our paintings,
our books, so many no one could have the same
(mathematics would show this usefully),
our choices, whether we care about dust
or gardens, our culinary interests.

However ubiquitous the chair and table,
our distribution of objects is our own,
collections too, pieces of what we meet
rescued as evidence of how our minds see
the possibly-shared world in public.

The inside of our house or head
is not for anybody. This new friend
is packing up his house to move.
He waves away Wittgenstein.
He's going to ride his horse
in the Netherlands.

Celestial Planisphere

a glow-in-the-dark jigsaw for ages 7+

Sarah Stewart

That box held the moon and the sun and more,
a stash that made you superheroic,
expert on constellations and the zodiac,
the universe studding your bedroom floor.
When it was finished you took it to school,
and everybody laughed. Of course you knew
the danger signs (*hide box! abort mission now!*)
but you stood firm till one of them shoved you.
Crash landing, a hard concrete collision;
stars exploding in your field of vision,
the brute taste of loss in your mouth
as you spat out blood and a wobbly tooth.
Somebody's mum hauled you to your feet.
Galaxies had shifted. Your voyage was complete.

Too to be true

Laura Tansley

When we were fifteen Tina dunked her left tit in a bowl of water to test if it was bigger than the other. In the middle of a corpsing night this gold crown, a b-cup trophy bud, was dipped and left to drip the proof.

They called us good girls because it turns out all the attention we needed on our unevenness was from each other and Archimedes. His hands, palimpsests of myth-rituals spilling all over the kitchen counter, reminded us of our perfect lack of symmetry and how witnessing ourselves was impossible.

We blamed our inability to hold it in on the dog, our habits on history, and boys for turning out our insides by closing their fusiform and face-blind eyes so they could corroborate the size.

Why He Did It

Rachel Rankin

I wonder why he did it?
Well, ah wisnae keepin' score.
Ah just know he wis here yisterday
an' he isnae here nae more.

I wonder what his thoughts were?
Mate, ye hardly caught em blinkin'.
It isnae as if he spoke aw eh time -
who knew wit the fuck he wis thinkin'?

I wonder how he felt that day?
He didnae come tae school.
Ah remember cuz ah wis lookin' fur him
an' ah looked like a right fuckin' tool.

I wonder if he felt the pain?
Well, where he fell wis grassy,
but we'd play-fight aw eh time
an' he'd be greetin' lit a lassie.

I wonder why he did it?
Mate, yer fuckin' killin' ma buzz.
Let's talk aboot suhin' else ya bam –
it's nuhin' tae dae wae us.

Bringing up the Bodies

Beloved Poison
ES Thompson

Constable, RRP £13.99, 400pp

The thing about contemporary novels set in the Victorian era is that you seldom encounter a slim one. So many of the satisfactions of books such as Michel Faber's *The Crimson Petal and the White* or Sarah Waters' *Fingersmith* are bound up with an amplitude of characters and detail as they are with reimagining the hackneyed view of Victorians as a moral and buttoned-up lot.

ES Thompson's *Beloved Poison*, a mystery novel set in the crumbling hospital of St Saviour's in a filthy, foggy London, is similarly crammed, by the dead as well as the living. The hospital is to be demolished to make way for a railway bridge, and the ancient graveyard at its centre is to be emptied of generations of human remains. A previous flood had revealed the extent of the problem:

"... scouring away the thin layer of soil that covered the most recent incumbents, packed beneath, one on top of the other, like kippers in a smokehouse. Bodies were churned into view: skulls, limbs, ribs and vertebrae sieved against the gates of the graveyard as the water rose... and receded."

Our guide through this charnel house setting is Jem Flockhart, the hospital apothecary, who has lived her life in male disguise as the only way to follow her father's trade. In the old chapel of the hospital, Jem and her new friend Will discover six miniature coffins containing eerie effigies. Their find sets in motion a quest with fatal consequences, for the eager anatomists of St. Saviour's have much to hide.

ES Thompson is a medical historian, and she uses her knowledge to furnish the book with a wealth of arcane poisons and alarming procedures, including a public amputation and the practices of the "resurrectionists", or body snatchers, who serviced doctors with subjects for dissection. So many of her references reminded me of true-life parallels from Edinburgh – the miniature coffins that were found in a cave on Arthur's Seat; James Miranda Barry, the Edinburgh-educated doctor discovered to be a woman on his deathbed; the Burke and Hare murders – that it was a certain relief when the plot led in that geographical direction.

The novel teems with sensory horrors and grotesquery in a manner that owes more to Penny Dreadfuls than to Dickens – the pox-ridden whorehouse, the walled asylum, the swamp-like slums and above all, the claggy bonepit that provides a wildly operatic climactic scene. Dank, gothic and grisly, Thompson musters familiar elements with such relish and momentum that a certain black comedy peeks through the criminal doings.

At times, the momentum and the descriptive detail can feel a touch overwhelming, the foreshadowing heavy-handed. Like a period parlour overcrowded with whatnots and antimacassars, the novel would benefit from a bit less of everything, a bit more air. As *Beloved Poison* is intended as the first of a series featuring the likeable Jem, it may settle into a more confident pace. Unlike the bone piles of St. Saviour's, the foundations are strong.

–The Gammy Bird

A well-dressed man disguise

Paragraphs at the end of the World
Graham Fulton

Penniless Press, RRP £6.99, 145pp

Graham Fulton serves up 115 razor-sharp paragraphs of auto-biographical observation on "whatever it is that makes existence tick." These seemingly random paragraphs are grouped into twelve sections with titles such as 'is this what the end of the world will look like?', 'a deliberate quality of heightened emptiness' and 'geological upthrust for our entertainment'. The sentence style is one of minimalist punctuation and precise imagery. Not a single word wasted, it's a kind of distilled Raymond Carver with the tone of a Scottish Alan Bennett. Part diary, part travelogue, part auto-biography *Paragraphs at the end of the World* is a meditation on mortality, memory and meaning, as here in the paragraph entitled 'crop':

"Standing motionless in a field of corn in Indiana. Just inside the edge with the giant dry stalks and leaves far above my head and the bluest sky and I seem to be almost vanishing, sinking away beyond the world. The end of the world is happening all the time. It's always here. The spinning away of spores of memory. Moments. Memorials. I seem to be becoming part of nothing. Leaving my selfish self behind. A field of dreams. A corn ghost. A small smile on my small face."

This is weighty subject matter which somehow floats in the spaces of a consciousness adorned with an absurd joy in life's small pleasures, which ameliorate the horrors and the terrors, and give resilience to our beating human hearts.

Fulton explores childhood memories and re-visits at least three of his earlier poems, 'Compactor Room', 'Marathon' and 'McDade R. Woodside Crematorium 10.30 a.m.' The latter two poems appeared first in the 1987 pamphlet *Tower of Babble*. The 'Compactor Room' resurfaces here in the paragraph 'breathe through your mouth' and for this reviewer it resonates strongly with Bohumil Hrabal's small masterpiece *Too Loud a Solitude*. Indeed, throughout the work there is a distrust of official systems and religious dogmas,

"This is the person, this measure of ash. We keep them alive until we can no longer come. It's all that can be done. Ritual from a time before religion was invented. Honest. Untouched."

I suspect what Fulton is getting at is that we should take the good in life and venerate and respect it: we're all simply, funnily, infuriatingly human regardless of religion, race or nation, and we're all heading for the same place.

Everything you'd expect from a collection of Fulton's poems is contained here but in a slightly different way: more considered, less emphatic. He is a man of quirky obsessions and they are still here, found objects, music, B-movies, outer-space... (Paisley has twenty three telephone boxes, all of which have been photographed and documented in Fulton's recent pamphlet *Twenty Three Telephones*.) There are also moments of marvellously bizarre humour in 'don't you fucking look at me' and 'face'. A wonderfully rewarding read.

—*Towser*

Portrait of an Artist

Dirt Road
James Kelman

Canongate, RRP £16.99, 369 pp

As *Dirt Road* starts, sixteen-year-old Murdo and his dad Tom catch the ferry to the mainland. His classmates are going to school but he is off to America – Glasgow to Memphis, Tennessee. An invitation from Tom's Uncle John and Aunt Maureen in Alabama is about to take them on a road trip through the American South. Murdo reckons it's "the best thing ever could have happened."

The worst has already. His big sister Eilidh died seven years back, aged just twelve, his mother a few months ago. A cancer affecting only the female line hit them each "like a bullet from a gun." Fine one minute, the next:

"... lying there on a hospital bed... nothing to be done... Males cannot help. All they can do is be there and be supportive. What else? Nothing, there is nothing."

Unsure whether the break is two weeks or nearly three, he thinks going away forever would be fine, to America sure, or wherever. At home, things closed in. "People die and you cannot do a thing."

Despite such massive loss, this is an incredibly warm novel, with the uneasy, yet quietly affectionate father-son relationship played out mostly in what they don't say as they spend time with their relatives, visit a Highland Gathering in Alabama, niggle and argue, while Murdo wracks his brain about how to persuade his dad to let him play a music festival in Louisiana with people he's just met. For above all, this is a portrait of a young artist – a gentle musician. It's a pleasure being inside Murdo's head in that way Kelman writes so distinctively and believably, immersed in the meanderings of a teenage consciousness, his awakening attraction to girls, how he knows and often points out right from wrong, in discussions on race, emigration and the relative likelihood of getting shot by the police. Murdo prefers to stay quiet about his grief, but enjoys his aunt's affection and determinedly sticks up for his mum and sister when he feels one or other is misrepresented.

He has a talent for the accordion, but hasn't played since his mother died. She had been the one supporting and encouraging him, taking him to band practices. On their second day a chance encounter with a young shopgirl, Sarah, leads to him meeting her grandmother, retired now, but a former Queen of Zydeco music

– a mix of blues, R&B and local music, originating from French speaking Creoles in Louisiana. Queen Monzee-ay spots the boy's interest and urges him to play at an impromptu session on the family's porch. Murdo grins when Sarah seeks him out with an invitation to join them performing in Lafayette in a fortnight, his ears zinging with happiness at her attention, at her rubbing his shoulder. She's beautiful and she touched him, but he almost instantly prepares for disappointment.

"... with Dad it would never happen. Never ever... What did he feel right at this very moment? Life was ending or something... It was gone and that was that. Only sometimes, Why me? That was what ye thought. Ye meet people and they have lives, but you don't."

Kelman's beautiful portrayal of the dilemma Murdo and his father face will deservedly bring him many new readers, as will the forthcoming film Dirt Road to Lafayette, directed by Kenny Glenaan, to whom the book is dedicated. A true artist, like Kelman, has core self-belief. A moving scene showing Murdo with that inner confidence is perfectly conceived in their ever changing, nuanced, and now threatened, relationship.

–*Fiona Montgomery*

Velo-city

Devil Take the Hindmost
Martin Cathcart Froden

Freight, RRP £9.99, 272pp

First of all, the bikes. Martin Cathcart Froden has saturated his first novel with the observations of an enthusiast's eye. He spends a lot of time on the details of the bikes – top tubes, glossy finishes, different kinds of pedals – and on the way they move, what he calls "the melody of mechanisms and merchandise": the "pattern of the spokes" as a bike speeds up, the intricacies of a velodrome race undertaken at 50 mph, the way Paul, the protagonist, weaves in and out of horses and carts as he makes deliveries around London. Over the course of the novel, Froden curates a collector's litany: "a 1921 Iver Johnson Special'; the red BSA Path Racer Paul spots in the street: 'look at the sloping head tube, that's lovely. Good quality steel."

For the cycling fan, this would be welcome whatever era the novel described. But it's useful here beyond its appeal to cyclists because it builds up a picture of London in the late 1920s. Froden uses Paul's day job delivering packages for the gangster Mr Morton, and the bike trips around London this job necessitates, as a way of depicting the bike as a technology somewhere between horses and carts and the motorcar. At one moment early in the book, Paul is caught up in a crash with a horse and cart and is pulled along the street. In terms of the plot this crash initiates his meeting with the beautiful Miriam, but it is also a moment that registers a city faced with technological change.

The bike's central position in this history is not limited to the effects this new machine has on its environment. Froden is aware of how the bike changed how human beings thought of themselves. Paul's fixer and minder Silas sees cyclists "as horses, dogs, cocks – animals, plain and simple. Speaking animals." Rather than a regression, though, this de-humanising aspect of cycling has more in common with the modernists' fascination with cycling as a blurring of animality (human or otherwise) and non-human machine-like efficiency. The Italian Futurists, for example, were attracted to cycling for precisely this reason, cycling as a perfect meshing of man and machine, the way it creates a kind of cyborg.

Froden is also aware of cycling's historical class position in England. For a lot of the sport's history, it has been a working-class sport centred as much on local velodromes as roads, and the novel takes its title from the Elimination Race, where riders zooming around a velodrome fight not to be the last over the line at timed intervals. Froden's depiction of this working-class world, with its gangsters, gambling and racketeering, is what in the blurbs gains the book comparisons to Graham Greene's *Brighton Rock*, and they're not wrong. But there's also a noir-ish edge to the narrative voice, which alternates between Silas' first person accounts and the more distanced perspective of Paul. The inhabitants of a London identified through its eel-and-mash shops and fruit and veg sellers are described in language that sounds like it's being spoken by a pulp fiction detective: "she's half spun sugar, half pickaxe." This wry vividness works well, especially in tandem with Froden's evocation of the dingy weirdness of underground London – a boarding house with doors that open onto nothing except a three-floor abyss, Mr Morton's bar that has "floorboards painted white and red, like a bleeding zebra." Froden has done a difficult thing with this novel; he's made us see London anew – from atop the bike's saddle.

– *Mark West*

La Isla Bonita

The Book Of Iona: An Anthology
Ed. *Robert Crawford*

Polygon Books, RRP £14.99, 306 pp

If you didn't know that Robert Crawford, the editor of *The Book Of Iona: An Anthology*, was one of the foremost academics in the field of Scottish writing, you would soon guess. There is an academic rigour in evidence, married to what feels like a literary obsession, which is admirable, and initially perhaps a little daunting. The writing includes poetry, prose, essays and other non-fiction, and stretches from the sixth century to the twenty-first, including works in Latin and Gaelic as well as Scots and English. In my ignorance, I believed an anthology of writing focusing on Iona would be a thin tome, but this is not only a comprehensive collection, but also eclectic and expansive. Crawford has not restricted himself and, as a good editor should, he has been brave and bold in his decisions.

A quick look at the contents pages offers up modern and contemporary writers such as Candia McWilliam, Edwin Morgan, Mick Imlah, David Kinloch, and Meg Bateman, as well as work from Crawford himself. It is in the present day writing that my own highlights from the anthology are to be found. Alice Thompson's 'Hologram' is a slice of magical realism which, like the anthology, is run through with religion, philosophy, and mysticism. Sara Lodge's 'The Grin Without A Cat' is about obsession and art, and is such a sensual piece of writing as to be tangible. It is possibly the best short story I have read this year.

But the more eye-catching, and dare I say interesting, names whose work appears in *The Book Of Iona* are those from the past, many of whom are as unexpected as they are exciting. Adomnan was an Abbot of Iona Abbey and is best known as the biographer of St Columba, the Irish monk who set up a monastery on the island in 563AD, so it is perhaps unsurprising that his work appears. The presence of Scottish literary legends Walter Scott, Robert Louis Stevenson, George Buchanan and James Boswell are arguably even more predictable, but welcome all the same as they include lesser-known work by all.

However, my eye was immediately drawn to writing by William Wordsworth, John Keats, Thomas Pennant, Herman Melville, and even Queen Victoria. Crawford allows us just a glimpse of 'how others see us', and this is not only informative

for this collection, but is something of which other editors of such anthologies should take note. Writers writing about home are only half the picture. A visitor's viewpoint is just as valid. Crawford's own poem 'Iona', and the fact it sits across the page from one ascribed to the aforementioned Saint Columba, lends the collection a nice symmetry, bringing together the past and the present as well as the editor and earliest named contributor.

It so happened that while reading *The Book Of Iona* I began another anthology of Scottish writing, one that is also based on place, *Umbrellas Of Edinburgh: Poetry and Prose Inspired by Scotland's Capital City*. While quite individual undertakings, it is informative to consider the two together and what they tell us about a wider national literature. The capital city and one of Scotland's more remote islands – in these two places extremes meet, and anthologies such as these help give us a clearer and more insightful picture of Scotland than we had previously. *The Book Of Iona* shows just what an anthology can achieve when approached with an open mind and imagination.

– Alistair Braidwood

Hot Air

The Aeronaut's Guide to Rapture
Stuart Campbell

Sandstone, RRP £8.99, 323pp

Stuart Campbell's second novel opens on its author narrowly missing a ride in a hot air balloon. "How could I write about balloons if I had never been on one?" he asks, pining after method writing authenticity He then proceeds to tell three tales which span the experiences of a woman down and out in 1870s Paris, a G.I. stranded in Vietnam 1965, and a priest falling foul of Sicily's present-day mafia. Each story is so pumped full to bursting with rich detail, one has to assume Campbell is either a *very* gifted researcher or has led a very interesting life.

The first tale is unashamedly picaresque and sees both Paris and its protagonist under siege: the city kettled by the Prussians, Ursule on the run from an abusive husband. No sooner have new outlandish characters appeared than you feel the air rush to fill their absence. The villain Gerard is irredeemable, Ursule's desire for her distant young love Louis infallible. It's either exhilarating or exhausting, depending on your tolerance for the genre's quirks.

The second story, of Dexter, sole survivor of a military plane crash, now pinned in place by a sheer cliff on one side and a crippling fear of a river on the other, finds originality in upending the Vietnam war narrative. Dexter's flashbacks are less concerned with the atrocities of war than his childhood on Coney Island, and his conversations with the corpses of his superiors are the only thing keeping him sane, as his memory dances around the tragic origin of his aquaphobia. Dark as this sounds, Campbell's perpetual touch of whimsy and the genuinely likeable protagonist make this a deeply engaging exploration of guilt, loneliness, desperation and ingenuity.

Finally, the third instalment, where a geriatric and less-than-holy priest slips from grace first into a daftly awkward sex-caper and then, jarringly, deep into Noir Italiano, could crudely be described as Father Ted meets The Godfather. Though Father Dante's the most complex and nuanced protagonist on offer, so focused is Campbell on unpacking the grand themes of rapture, escape and redemption, it's difficult not to sympathise when Eleonora, Dante's femme fatale, exclaims "Oh for God's sake, Father, kiss me, I'm getting bored."

Yet, *The Aeronaut's Guide to Rapture* is a virtuoso endeavour. To dip into several different genres so completely and in some cases subvert them, comes with the risk of losing a few readers along the way. And though the book has flaws, Campbell himself is only too eager to point them out. The author-narrator reappears in brief interludes to pick apart his own stories: this part too whimsical, that part too out-of-character, even going so far as to doubt the relevance of the book's core concepts. As the author-narrator also eventually abandons his writerly concerns with the aid of a balloon flight, the structure suggests all three stories have something greater to say as a whole.

But in truth this meta-narrative unintentionally pushes you to look for fault in the telling, and undercuts the charm of the individual works. Most glaring of all, to varying degrees each story leaves their protagonist up in the air, if not always literally. This is, perhaps, the point: nobody's life ever wraps up neatly, and we would do well to grab every chance at escapism that comes our way, consequences be damned. Though the mind aches for resolution, there is no coming back to earth.

– *Dangerous Beans*

The Very Image of Life

Settle
Theresa Munoz

Vagabond Voices, RRP £8.95, 66 pp

Percy Shelley wrote in *A Defence of Poetry* "A poem is the very image of life expressed in its eternal truth." The line came back to me while reading Theresa Munoz's powerful collection, Settle. With the Prime Minister talking of using immigrants as 'bargaining chips' in Brexit negotiations, Munoz's direct, subtle poetry brings the everyday back to detached discussions of migration. In the two sequences that make up this book, we find the "very image of life" as experienced by those at the sharp end of an all-too-blunt debate.

The first, *Settle*, deals with the poet's experiences as the child of Filipino immigrants in Canada and as an immigrant herself in Scotland. One always hesitates to assume that the 'I' of poetry is the poet speaking directly to the reader, but given how exactly the poems map onto Munoz's biography – as outlined in the concluding essay 'Coming to Scotland' – I feel it's safe to describe this collection as autobiographical.

Many of the poems are vignettes focusing on one specific experience – racism, visa applications, homesickness – while the rest unpack the spiritual experience of migration, often by comparison with those of her parents'. In all, it is Munoz's eye for a telling detail that arrests the reader, such as the dropped payslip in opening poem 'Twenty-two' or the uncomfortable security pat-down in 'Travelling'. Each poem grows from these commonplace images into poignant elucidations of an aspect of migration, the sequence building crystalline into a self-portrait of the artist as an outsider.

In one standout poem, 'For Me', the reader gets to vicariously live the warm, almost Dickensian glow that a throwaway part of speech can give the lonely, the isolated.

"Could you type your pin for me.

Just a phrase, but the same phrase
at the shoe place, post office too.
For me... those words hold
a petal-like intimacy,
a light friendship"

These poems remind us that when we talk of immigrants, we are never discussing statistics or trends, we are talking about people with hopes, fears and human fragility. A poem like 'For Me' allows access to that reality better than any op-ed, think-piece or debate ever could. What a difference it would make if every episode of Question Time began and ended with a snapshot like this. These poems should be taught in our schools.

The second sequence, *Digital Life*, stands in contrast to the first. While the voices of Settle are often out of their depth and lost, the poet finds herself much more at home online. The style and tone of the poems shift accordingly. The autobiographical thread continues but we are in new poetic terrain with more found poetry and experimentation. Humour runs throughout the collection but whereas in Settle it tends to the bittersweet, here is it more cynical and playful, such as in 'Junk', built out of a scam email promising friendship and riches in exchange for "the number of your safe foreign account".

But there's loneliness here too. In 'Her favourite email' Theresa (named in the poem) sits on a bus in Scotland rereading an email "from a friend across the ocean". The depth of friendship stretched over thousands of miles rises from prosaic questions such as "How are you getting on?" and helps to "smooth over a bad day". In Digital Life we are never truly alone, but it's never quite enough. As it says in 'Refresh'

"Each furious click
in the slow spell of night
means there's a missing
part of her life, beyond
these tiny words lost
in empty white."

–Iain Maloney

A Masterful Learner

The Campbill Wren
James McGonigal

Red Squirrel Press, RRP £8.99, 80 pp

It is hard to believe that *The Camphill Wren* is James McGonigal's first book-length collection, given that he has kept up a strong poetic presence for nearly two decades through a series of elegant and craftsman-like pamphlets. It is also difficult to easily distil just what this book is about, considering its themes – from elegies for older poets such as Kirkpatrick Dobie and Edwin Morgan, through events like the Troubles to poems on the experience of adjusting to retirement – are wide-ranging. However, reading this collection, it is easy to detect McGonigal's signature style that combines both a lightness and deftness of touch with an emotional and existential heft. Take for instance, 'Essentialist' from the 'Abandoned Language' sequence, which is all about the speaker's struggle to recall certain things. Out of the seeming dimness comes a crystalline memory of his daughter:

"If you meet me and have
            some claim
    to be my daughter

    allow me to think of the
        shades and lengths
    of your hair over several
                    winters."

Perhaps the most winning aspect of McGonigal's poetry, amply evidenced here, is its capacity and desire to learn, even from the perspective of retirement. He confesses to be haunted by his father, and many poems contain lines such as those in 'Understudy' where the speaker is "studying for the role of my father / and found hesitations". In 'Learning Cloud' the speaker bemoans their poor hearing and that they're losing the wonder of birdsong only to seek to replace this pleasure of the past with "learning cloud", or the language of weather and how to speak it. While McGonigal sometimes overdoes it a little on the Michael Longley-esque mock-heroic portraits of the writer in old age, with mug of tea and notebook, wearing fuddy-duddy Marks and Spencer socks and slacks (see 'Left-Right Coalition Set to Fall'), he also shares with Longley a fascination for the elements, for water, wind and cloud and is often to be caught rehearsing his own death, as in 'Regarding Water':

"I want to die looking at
water
I want to die having regard
to water
whose wrinkled face is supple
for its age
I want to die smiling kindly
on water."

At their best, these poems are conflicted between a desire for domestic comfort and a restless intellectual and experiential search for something new. There is much talk of cloud and a looking up to the skies because, like Edwin Morgan in old age, McGonigal is beginning to free himself of certain burdens, so his mood and spirit can lift. In 'Getting On' he finds his life written down in the phrases of a French grammar book published the year he was born, but is still keen to get on with his "homework". For all of his self-identification as a learner, McGonigal is a master of the arresting poetic turn of phrase. Take, for instance, the line in 'Low Country and Western' where a "bed" is "a desk where love is written and re-read". Finally, the key to this collection seems to be in the title poem, 'The Camphill Wren', where McGonigal shows us that we must learn to look and then look again:

"Once-in-a-decade sightings
made me think that the wren
was declining –
but no, Gerry says: only for
years I've had my eye
on other things."

–*Richie McCaffery*

Not One Racist Bone

The Empathetic Store
Jackie Kay

Mariscat Press, RRP £6, 36 pp

Jackie Kay's highly accessible style has the effervescence of song: there is anger, delicacy, love, tenderness, heartbreak and resilience in these poems. She knows exactly when to be crisp, succinct and minimal, and when to let the language expand into a less precise, more expansive and impressionistic view. I sensed echoes of Burns, Tom Leonard and W. S. Graham in the mix here.

'A Lang Promise' is about the endurance and resilience of relationships, perhaps between parents and children, or between lifelong lovers. It is delivered to us in a musical mixture of Scots and English that flies from the page and heads toward song,

> "Whether the weather be
> dreich or fair, my luve,
> [...]
> I'll carry ma lantern and daur
> defend ye agin ony enemy;
> and whilst there is breath in
> me, I'll blaw it intae ye.
> Fir ye are ma true luve, the
> bonnie face I see afore me;
> nichts I fall intae slumber, it's
> ye I see swimmingly—
> all yer guidness and blitheness,
> yer passion."

'Extinction' has a blend of anger, irony and humour often found in Tom Leonard's work. It uses repetition, alliteration and sound to great effect revealing a sense of a broad political struggle; cultural, economic and global. Kay embraces the idea of 'equal but different' with seriousness, depth and respect. Racism, in all its forms, is strongly challenged in this poetry: "We closed the borders, folks, we nailed it. / No trees, no plants, no immigrants."

'Would Jane Eyre Please Come to the Information Desk?' and 'Here's my Pitch' also challenge racism. These poems do not preach but describe. And for these pieces alone this pamphlet is worth reading.

There is, however, much more besides. 'Rannoch River' is a beautiful tribute to the author's father, itself "eloquent, articulate, certain, clear". It carries us into the final section of the pamphlet 'The Ardtornish Quintet', a wonderfully reflective and meditative sequence on memory, time,

love and life that is both highly personal and universal. It has echoes of Graham's 'The Nightfishing', with its superbly simple opening lines: "Very gently struck / The quay night bell."

Kay, however, takes us into her childhood and her 'nostalgia': it is a fascinating journey out to the Scottish West at Loch Aline. The Lochaline General Stores is 'The Empathetic Store' of the pamphlet title and serves as metaphor for the good that comes from human-contact, sociability and community. Finally, there is another layer of meaning too, which relates to the life of a human consciousness in a particular place, and explores how place, individual and community interact to give us our cultures, our families and friends, our lives and our memories:

> "Here, on the other side,
> across the water
> the light is leaving the sky,
> pink and blushing,
> like a slow ballet dancer's
> last pirouette.
> There's a glimmer like hope
> before it cools.
> I walk past the fish nets
> bundled like lost souls,
> and head round the corner to
> the light"

—Towser.

The Best Things in Life Are Not Things

Waking at Five Happens Again
Alison Prince

Happenstance/Mariscat, RRP £10.00, 76 pp

This collection reminds me of the old adage: 'the best things in life are not things'. Alison Prince has distilled into this collection so many best non-things from a richly-lived life. In the opening poem, 'Reckoning', we are faced with the impossibility of accounting what is really valuable: "There is no column in which to enter / sudden rainbows". Perhaps it is poetry's unique role to gesture towards those elements of our experience that words can barely capture, and which could certainly never be recorded in a spreadsheet.

Alison Prince finds gold dust in the most banal-seeming events. Take this early morning bus-ride from her home, on the Isle of Arran, down to the harbour:

> "Doors have hissed shut.
> The insect bus
> creeps on towards Brodick,
>   while outside
> dawn tears the black sky open
> like a tangerine."

We come to understand, while reading, that this heightened sense of the wonder in the world is the result of the poet living precariously with bad health. She sometimes must complain about the agony of long waits for medical attention, but meanwhile, there are miracles – waking

at five again is one of them, so is "the bread knife, [...] newly well-known to the hand" – and riches, like the "full-ripe pear turned from laburnum wood" given to her by a wood-turner she met in the post office and offered a felled tree from her garden. The connection to Midas, for whom everything turned to gold, is unspoken.

The poet has had both a full and a long life, as shown by vivid memories of World War 2 bomb shelters, and the deaths of people who did not reach them in time. She expresses an acceptance of mortality, and gratitude for having lived long, through the memory of the death in a bombing raid of a neighbouring girl, younger than her, to whom she had given her doll. This could have been her. It could have been any of us.

The sequence of poems sometimes feels vertiginous, tumbling from the concerns of present day old age to fragments of early childhood experience, but isn't this the nature of memory? Throughout it all, a sense of the bravery and kindness of the poet builds.

Compassion is evident in plenty. One of the best poems shows a classroom where the tough kid Jimmy waves a gun, and then, later, falls and hits his head and cries, inconsolably, while she, and the other children, "get on quietly." The difficult parts of life are shown, unadorned, without sentimentality and often with black humour, including a gun-toting husband who echoes the brutalized child.

Alison Prince is a feisty, positive, intelligent, honest writer and her poems are full of life-affirming wisdom. She says she missed the boat, but found joy anyway,

down on the beach, paddling, where
the cold sea-water on bare feet connects
childhood memories to the still intense
experience of mature years:

>"it shocks again
>as it did only yesterday
>when your soft-padded feet
>were still growing."

Our days may be numbered, but their
nanoseconds are shining.

–Mandy Haggith

In Memoriam:
'Dear Gutter'
2014-2017
She is survived by a widow paragraph.
A private committal will be held next
Tuesday.
No flowers.

Contributor Biographies

JD Allan is a musician, singer-songwriter, writer and former member of noughties Glaswegian rock band The Blimp.

DM Black is a poet, reviewer and psychoanalyst. He has published five poetry collections and various books on psychoanalysis and religion.

William Bonar was shortlisted in 2015 for a New Writers Award. His award winning pamphlet, *Offering*, is available at www.redsqirrelpress.com

John Boursnell is a writer and artist living in Glasgow.

Alistair Braidwood runs the Scottish cultural website Scots Whay Hae! and his reviews are found in the more discerning publications.

Nick Brooks is a novelist and poet, currently based in Slovakia. He's authored three novels and a collection of poems.

Paul Brownsey lives in Bearsden. Most of Scotland's literary magazines have published stories by him, and Lethe Press, New Jersey, USA, published a whole book of them, *His Steadfast Love and Other Stories*.

Thomas Clark is a writer from Glasgow. He is currently poet-in-residence at Selkirk FC and Scots co-editor at Bella Caledonia.

AC Clarke's latest collections are *A Natural Curiosity,* (New Voices Press), shortlisted for the 2012 Callum Macdonald Award, and *Fr Meslier's Confession* (Oversteps Books). She is currently working on a fourth collection.

Beth Cochrane is co-host and co-curator of the spoken word night, Interrobang! She works in an art library and has Twitter: **@literature_wine**

Claire Deans Donnelly was born in Glasgow, and now lives and works in Vietnam. She has previously published a few poems, and won a short story competition.

Ever Dundas is a writer specialising in the weird and macabre. Her first novel, *Goblin,* will be published by Freight in May 2017.

Paul Éluard French surrealist trailblazer. Stalinist. Dead. Tubercular barbecue.

Sally Evans's latest pamphlet *Anderson's Piano* reached No.1 in the Amazon women's poetry bestseller list as an e-book.

Jim Ferguson lives and writes in Glasgow. He is the author of several books. See his website at **www.jimfergusonpoet.co.uk**

Graham Fulton is the author of over fifteen pamphlets and six poetry collections, the latest of which is *One Day in the Life of Jimmy Denisovich* from Smokestack Books. **www.grahamfulton-poetry.com**

Harry Giles is a performer, poet, and general doer of things. He grew up in Orkney, Scotland, and now lives in Edinburgh.

Gavin Gilmour writes screenplays, plays and prose fiction. He lives in Aberdeen.

Benjamin Guérin is a poet and ceramicist. His first book, *Métropole Oubliée,* was published in October 2016 by Lucie Éditions. See: **nousatelier.blogspot. fr** and **facebook.com/nousatelier**

Marilyn Hacker is the author of thirteen books of poems, and fourteen collections of translations of French and Francophone poets. *DiaspoRenga*, a collaborative sequence written with the poet Deema Shehabi, was published in 2014. She lives in Paris.

Diana Hendry's most recent poetry collection is *The Seed-Box Lantern* (Mariscat). Due in April, *My Father as an Ant* – short stories (Red Squirrel Press).

Doug Johnstone is an author, journalist and musician. He's written eight novels, his latest being *Crash Land*, umpteen short stories, five albums and two EPs.

Vénus Khoury-Ghata is a Lebanese poet, novelist and long-time Paris resident, the author of twenty-two novels, and eighteen collections of poems. Five collections of her poems and one novel are available in English. Recipient of the Académie Française prize in poetry in 2009, she was named an Officer of the Légion d'Honneur the following year. *A Handful of Blue Earth*, is released in 2017.

Jonathan Lamy is a multidisciplinary poet and performer. He holds an interdisciplinary PhD from University of Québéc at Montréal and has published three collections of poetry at Editions du Noroit.

Aurelia Lassaque is a bilingual poet in French and Occitan. Interested in the interaction between various forms of art, she often cooperates with visual artists, videomakers, dancers and particularly musicians. She will be reading and singing at StAnza in 2017.

Chin Li grew up in Hong Kong but has lived in Scotland for years, and has published works in *Glasgow Review of Books* and *Gnommero.*

Liz Lochhead is an award winning poet and playwright. She was Scotland's Makar (National Poet) from 2011-2016.

Shona MacLean lives in Ross-Shire and is the author of the 'Alexander Seaton' and 'Damian Seeker' historical crime novels.

Andrew McCallum lives and works in Biggar. He has visited the Scottish Parliament and was not impressed.

Rachel McCrum is a poet and performer, working somewhere between Edinburgh and Montreal. Her first collection *The First Blast To Awaken Women Degenerate* is due out from Freight Books in summer 2017.

Ronnie McCluskey is currently seeking agent representation for his first novel.

Olivia McMahon has two published poetry collections and is working on a third. She also writes novels.

Chris McQueer is a 25 year old writer and sales assistant from the east end of Glasgow.

Gordon Meade lives and writes in Fife. His next collection, *The Year of The Crab*, will be published in 2018 by Cultured Llama Publishing.

Gillian Mellor can sometimes be found in The Moffat Bookshop re-arranging the window.

Fiona Montgomery, a graduate of Glasgow University's Creative Writing MLitt, is a freelance journalist and is writing a memoir.

Stephen Nelson's books include *Lunar Poems for New Religions* (KFS), *Thorn Corners* (erbacce) and *Arcturian Punctuation* (Xexoxial).
www.afterlights-vispo.tumblr.com.

Melody Nixon is a writer, editor, and artist currently living in the Scottish Borders. **www.melodynixon.com**

Marek O Lasce is both a novelist and a veteran of such theatre companies as 7:84(Scotland), Wildcat and The Tron.

Stuart A Paterson born 1966, lives by the Solway Coast, walks alot. His 2016 collection *Border Lines* won the Saboteur Award.

Nalini Paul's poetry explores shifting identities and 'natural' landscapes. She has collaborated with visual artists, musicians and dancers; and is currently working on a project for the stage. **www.nalinipaul.com**

Rachel Plummer is a poet based in Edinburgh. In 2016 she won a Scottish Book Trust New Writers Award.

Jon Plunkett lives and writes in Scotland. He is also founder of The Corbenic Poetry Path. More info: **www.corbenicpoetrypath.com**

Tom Pow is a poet and travelling writer. His mst recent storues are *In Another World – Among Europe's Dying Villages*, *A Wild Adventure – Thomas Watling, Dumfries Convict Artist* and *Concerning the Atlas of Scotland and other poems.*

Rachel Rankin is a reader and writer of poetry. She hopes to return to university in 2017 to study for a masters degree in creative writing.

James Robertson's novel *The Testament of Gideon Mack* was longlisted for the 2006 Booker Prize. His 2010 book *And the Land Lay Still,* received the Saltire Society Scottish Book of the Year award.

Calum Rodger is a Glasgow-based poet, performer and scholar. His pamphlet *Know Yr Stuff: Poems on Hedonism* is published by Tapsalteerie.

Andrew Rubens' collaborative translations with Henry King of Benjamin Fondane's poetry are published by NYRB this year.

Lou Sarabadzic was born in France and lives in England. She blogs at **predictedprose. com** and **telpere.com**. Her novel *La Vie verticale* was published in 2016. Her first poetry collection, *Ensemble*, won the Prix de la Crypte and will appear in 2017.

Cassie Smith-Christmas was raised in Virginia and Lives in Glasgow. She is a Gaelic-speaking academic by day, aspiring author by night, and is currently writing her first novel.

Elissa Soave writes poetry and short stories. Her work has appeared in *New Writing Scotland*, *Working Words* and *Freak Circus*.

Dan Spencer lives in Glasgow with his wife and daughters. He is published in *Gutter, Flash,* and *New Writing Scotland.*

Sarah Stewart is an Edinburgh-based writer. Her poems have appeared in *Anon, Mslexia, New Writing Dundee, The Pickled Body, The Scotsman* and *Best Scottish Poems 2014.*

Shane Strachan's work has appeared in *New Writing Scotland, Northwords Now, Causeway/Cabhsair,* Freight's *Out There* anthology and many other publications.

Laura Tansley lives in Glasgow. Her poems are forthcoming in *Tears in the Fence, Southword* and *Stand.* **@laura_tans**

James Thomas is a professional translator and a researcher in nineteenth- and twentieth-century Occitan literature. He is the translator of *Solstice and Other Poems: Poems in Occitan* by Aurélia Lassaque (2012).

Ryan Vance was the editor of *The Queen's Head* and is currently writing an eco-dystopian novel, with ghosts in. **www.ryanvance.co.uk**

Lynnda Wardle was born in Johannesburg and lives in Glasgow. She has appeared in *thi wurd, Gutter* and *NWS.* **lynndawardle.com**

Nuala Watt teaches at the University of Glasgow. Poems have appeared in *Jacket2* and in anthologies including *Be The First To Like This: New Scottish Poets* (Vagabond Voices 2014)

Mark West teaches at Glasgow University, edits *Glasgow Review of Books,* and writes for *3am Magazine, Review31,* and *The List.*

Nicola White is a writer and curator living in internal exile on the Clyde Coast. Her first novel, *In the Rosary Garden* won the Dundee International Book Prize.

Ali Whitelock, Scottish, living in Sydney. Her memoir, *Poking Seaweed with a Stick...* published by Polygon 2009. Her first poetry collection is now complete.

Christie Williamson is from Yell in Shetland and lives in Glasgow. His latest publication is *Oo an Feddirs* (Luath).